HUTCHY
MIRACLE MAN

HUTCHY
MIRACLE MAN
THE AUTOBIOGRAPHY

IAN HUTCHINSON
WITH TED MACAULEY

HUTCHY
MIRACLE MAN
THE AUTOBIOGRAPHY

IAN HUTCHINSON
WITH TED MACAULEY

JOHN BLAKE

Published by
John Blake Publishing Limited,
3 Bramber Court, 2 Bramber Road,
London W14 9PB, England

www.johnblakebooks.com

www.facebook.com/johnblakebooks ⬛
twitter.com/jblakebooks ⬛

First published in hardback in 2016

ISBN: 978-1-78606-123-2

British Library Cataloguing-in-Publication Data:
A catalogue record for this book is available from the British Library.

Design by www.envydesign.co.uk

Printed in Great Britain by CPI Group (UK) Ltd

3 5 7 9 10 8 6 4

Papers used by John Blake Publishing are natural, recyclable products
made from wood grown in sustainable forests. The manufacturing processes
conform to the environmental regulations of the country of origin.

Every attempt has been made to contact the relevant copyright-holders,
but some were unobtainable. We would be grateful if the appropriate people
could contact us.

CONTENTS

ACKNOWLEDGEMENTS

We, Ted Macauley and I, would like to express our gratitude to a motorbike-race-mad set of guys who were only too ready and eager to offer their support and know-how on our bumpy road to publication.

They are: F1 powerbroker Bernie Ecclestone; multiple MotoGP world champion Valentino Rossi; much-loved broadcaster Murray Walker, OBE; former *Motor Cycle News* boss Sir Robin Miller and his bike-writer son Brian; ex-MotoGP chief Paul Butler; writer Stu Barker; former British champion and TT winner Roger Burnett; Manx-based publicist Simon Crellin; and John Watterson, the Isle of Man newspaper's sports editor.

We also gratefully acknowledge Steve Parrish and Jamie Witham, Clive Padgett, Stuart Bland and Rick Broadbent.

Grateful thanks, too, to the many other family members, friends and supporters, too numerous to mention, without whom this book would not have been possible.

The publishers would also like to express their gratitude to Paul Knight, for proposing the idea of this book in the first place.

FOREWORD
BY VALENTINO ROSSI

I only found out what the TT really meant when I went there in 2009. You have to be there on that island to understand it. There's a different look to the racers there. I used to think they were crazy. But I later realised that there's a lot more to it than that. A certain craziness is just one of the elements you need to race on the Isle of Man. I have the great privilege to know Hutchy and thanks to him I grew to understand and appreciate the race even more. I've always admired Ian for his determination, which he never lost even during hard times. There is so much of him and so much of the TT in this book. In other words, it's a special book.

VALENTINO ROSSI

FOREWORD

BY MURRAY WALKER, OBE

For the whole of my long life I have been deeply involved with just about every type of motorsport from karts, 50cc racing motorcycles and motocross to touring and sports cars and Formula One. I`ve travelled the world to commentate on events as varied as the local Chinese heroes' race in Macau for 350cc Yamaha riders and the fabled twenty-four-hour sports car race at Le Mans, so I feel entitled to state that the greatest race of them all is the unique and historic Isle of Man TT.

Nowhere else offers the challenge of its 37.75 mile course on public roads, where the riders race their way through towns, villages and open countryside at over 200 mph and climb and descend 2,000 foot Mount Snaefell, with a mind-blowing average lap speed for the top men of over 130 mph.

To face and overcome the unique challenge of the TT you have to be very special indeed, and in the many years I have been there since I first went as a child in 1925 I've been lucky enough to see all the TT superstars in action, from Alec Bennett, Stanley Woods and Jimmy Guthrie to Joey Dunlop and John McGuinness, by way of Geoff Duke, John Surtees, Mike Hailwood and Giacomo Agostini. People argue endlessly about who was the greatest, but in my view you can only form a subjective opinion, bearing in mind the very different circumstances they competed in. Having said that, there's not a shadow of doubt that amongst them, for what he has achieved and the way he has achieved it, is Ian Hutchinson.

Yes, others have won more TTs than he has – a brilliant fourteen as I write, including that amazing 100 per cent 2010 record of five wins at a single TT meeting – but none have done so whilst overcoming the hideous results of the blameless racing accident which nearly resulted in Ian losing a leg, let alone the racing career which is the driving force of his life.

The Ian Hutchinson story which follows, co-authored by Ted Macauley, one of Britain's top sports writers, a close friend of the great Mike Hailwood and a man who has a deep affection for and knowledge of the TT, is one which can only generate respect and admiration for the skill, the bravery and the seemingly limitless determination of this quietly spoken Yorkshireman. He is a living example of how the human spirit can overcome the greatest of setbacks, and he is an inspiration to us all never to give up.

Just read on and you'll see what I mean.

MURRAY WALKER

CHAPTER 1

MANX MAGIC

Just to compete in the Isle of Man TT has to be one of the most exciting challenges a professional motorbike racer could ever face.

To complete the Snaefell Mountain course and overcome and outsmart the ever-present risk factor – to say nothing of the hundred or so committed rivals – and cross the line to finish in one piece is a triumph in itself.

To stand garlanded on one of the three platforms on the winners' podium opposite the main grandstand is a mind-blowing and memorable achievement. To win is, of course, every competitor's dream, unbelievably gratifying, wonderfully extra-special, a reward to cherish.

To do it fourteen times, with five victories in one week, as I have, is sheer unadulterated joy, an unsurmountable peak of satisfaction when you have readily and eagerly accepted and faced up to the perils of racing in all manner of difficult weather and in ever challenging and unpredictable track conditions, on the very brink of survival at more than 200 mph, often brushing shoulders with an equally determined, cold-eyed rival unwilling to surrender one inch of road and hell-bent on defending his hard-earned position in the race.

Let me set the scene that has historically intrigued, mesmerised, defeated, scared, tested to the extreme, and covered in glory legions of racers of all levels and standards, unbeatable world champions and no-hopers and also-rans alike, professional works riders with millions of pounds-worth of backing, teams of engineering expertise and mega sponsorships and, in complete and cruel contrast, the necessarily penny-careful privateers, who often have to stay up all night doubling as their own mechanics, tuning and tweaking mounts that they can only pray will at best complete at least one lap of the world's riskiest (but most rewarding, in terms of self-satisfaction) motorcycle racetrack.

Midway between England and Ireland in the Irish Sea, 80 miles from Liverpool, 66 miles from Belfast, is the self-governing British Crown dependency Isle of Man, Ellan Vannin, with a population of about 85,000 and inhabited since 6500 BC. The Queen is Head of State.

It is 30 miles long, 16 miles wide, 221.54 square miles in total, with as centrepiece Snaefell Mountain, measuring 2,034 feet, the high point of the circuit, taking in 688 miles of public roads, 37¾ of them making up each lap of the race, with 264 corners a circuit, forming the TT stage, and skirting the four main Manx towns: the capital, Douglas, Ramsey, Peel and Castletown.

The mainly holiday island's famous symbol is a triskelion, depicting three joined legs; its motto *Quocunque jeceris, stabit,* which, translated from the Latin, is 'Whithersoever you throw it, it will stand'.

That could well have been fashioned as the TT's very own upbeat message of defiance as it has survived triumphantly more than a hundred years of just about every drama and potential setback you could imagine could be hurled at it, with never a moment's doubt about its attraction as a challenge completely irresistible to fearless two-wheeled road racers who revel in its risks and the 50,000 or so enthusiasts who, rain or shine, make the annual pilgrimage to the island motorsport mecca. There, they watch for free from the closed public roads the daredevilry of TT legends, world champions and top-flight winners Mike Hailwood, Geoff Duke, Giacomo Agostini, Mick Grant, Phil Read, Roger Burnett, Alex George, Joey Dunlop, Charlie Williams and more lately the 'Morecambe Missile' John McGuinness, another multi-winner and as formidable a rival as it is possible to face.

There is never a moment of boredom either for fans or for us riders facing unnerving tests at every turn and hairpin, over every jump and switchback, hurtling at top speed along every hedge, pavement or wall-lined straight, while the roadsides are packed with viewers jostling for a close-up view of their favourites as they roar by.

With so many essentials and potential problems for the rider to remember and cope with in a split-second, the stress and pressure on every racer, whatever his skill, his level of experience, was and is paramount.

Ted Macauley, Hailwood's best friend and manager, recalls how Mike almost begged him and finally persuaded him, reluctant and apprehensively fearful as Ted was, to fix up a comeback for him in 1978.

'Mike, the absolute Mountain Circuit master with nothing to prove except to himself, became insolubly restless and he could not fend off his longing for a return and an escape, whatever the risks and potential damage, from the boredom of his life in New Zealand.

'He was thirty-nine years of age, pot-bellied and with an almost useless leg after being badly injured in an F1 crash at the fearsome Nürburgring track in Germany, which almost killed him, but left him instead crippled and limping. He told me he was bored to death, and he wrote to me asking me, in top secret, to organise a TT comeback – if they would have him! He certainly wasn't doing it for the money; he was a multimillionaire.

'He flew home to stay with me after the excited Auto Cycle Union and TT hierarchy had eagerly and enthusiastically welcomed his planned return, whatever his fee. Mike had not raced the island for more than a decade and he told me over dinner that he could not any longer fight off his burning desire to tackle the TT's irresistible challenge to his, albeit rusty, motorcycle racing ability and to see if he still had guts enough to do it flat-out against a hundred or so other guys. He emphasised he wanted not just to tour around among the also-rans but to give it his all and strive for victory. Even if the organisers didn't fancy paying him. But they did. And how!'

This is what Mike had to say about taking on the TT, skimming its stone walls, dodging seagulls, smoothing the inherited road traffic bumps and taking his bike to the limit both speed- and safety-wise. 'Everything happens so bloody quickly you don't have time to get scared.' I could not agree more.

And, typically, after his dramatic and amazing 1978 Formula One victory on a Ducati, his thirteenth TT win, in front of a sell-out, record-breaking crowd all thrilled to see the legend's reappearance, he added with a grin: 'And there was a cracking-looking blonde in black leathers in the crowd on the bend at Creg-ny-Baa.'

He gave Ted his rare and treasured winged Mercury silver trophy, awarded to TT winners, with, Ted says, the blessing: 'Thanks to you it all happened.'

The romance of his famed comeback aptly fitted the drama and development over the years of the TT's magical attraction to competitors only too eager put their skill and courage to the ultimate test for prize money comparatively small in contrast to funds offered elsewhere on safer short circuits.

My fellow Yorkshireman Mick Grant, who blitzed Hailwood's eight-year-old lap record TT record at a speed of 109.82 mph, and was a winner seven times out of sixteen TTs, recalled his tussle with Mike in their 1978 clash, by saying: 'When you race against men of his class you have to ensure you bring the best out of yourself and when you have to do it at a place like the TT when your nerve and your ability have to be at a constant high peak, the feeling of respect for its dangers and demands is almost beyond explanation. To be a winner there surmounts by far any success you might have had anywhere else. It really is that special.'

More than 250 riders – one of them a sidecar passenger, twenty-five-year-old Marie Lambert from Switzerland, who died from injuries suffered when her husband Claude crashed at the 35th Milestone in 1961 – have been killed tackling the treacherous up-hill-and-down-dale circuit on public roads.

Tragically, in 2005, the deadliest year in the history of the Mountain circuit, eleven people, including a marshal and a spectator, perished in the island's two motorcycle race events. In the late summer Manx Grand Prix, over the same course as the TT, heartbreakingly, six riders were killed.

Those figures do not take into account the 'Mad Sunday' dozens of fatalities when the reckless wannabees opt to take on the TT's dangers en masse when the track is open, albeit under heavy police surveillance, or those visiting bikers who fancy their chances as speed merchants only to suffer for their lack of good sense.

But, as Mick Grant, has said: 'The Mad Sunday lot, the ones who flagrantly chance their arm as opposed to those guys who only want sensibly to sample the circuit out of curiosity and are not out to prove they can go as quick as the professionals, are a danger to everybody else as well as themselves.

'As for that sad list of competitors who have gone home in a box, you can't allow yourself to dwell on those numbers who have perished over the years. In my case many of them were good friends built up in a long career of racing. And it has been a very sad tally. But they were all doing what they loved. Nobody forced them to race. They all felt, I am sure, that they had something to prove to themselves and anybody watching in support of their effort.'

Grand Prix superstar and twice world 500cc champion, Barry Sheene, a brilliantly talented rider and racing's glamour boy, opted to take on the TT at just about the height of his career – and crashed out, luckily unhurt, on the first serious but slowish corner, Quarter Bridge, a few seconds after being flagged away to start his hell-for-leather plunge down the fearsomely steep Bray Hill.

'At the TT I frightened the life out of myself and fell off at Quarter Bridge when the clutch grabbed and threw the back wheel out and the bike slid from under me. I was so lucky I wasn't hurt. But, anyway, after Bray Hill, that bloody scary drop right after the start, I had no real idea and hardly a clue what was happening to me or where I was going. It was like a madcap downhill slalom and I was all over the place on the dodgiest circuit in motorbike racing.

'I was thankful that I had fallen off where I did because, as I said at the time, if I had raced any further my crash might have happened somewhere else, far more dangerous, and I could have been seriously injured and knocked about a bit. That for me was the end of the TT. I had missed most of the practice sessions because I was late getting to the Isle of Man. By the time I took my place on the grid for the race I had done only eight laps – and, as any TT rider or fan knows, that is nowhere near enough time to commit all those corners and dodgy spots to memory and try to go flat out for a win or even to finish. So, quite honestly, I was a bit silly to even think about racing there. And I would strongly advise anybody, however good you think you are or whatever success you might have had elsewhere, don't be as daft as I was and imagine you can take it in your stride.

'But my admiration for all those hundreds of guys who, over the years and in all sorts of conditions, have given it their all, whatever the outcome, never faded. My personal experience was a bleeding nightmare.

'I hate the bloody place,' the embarrassed Suzuki ace exploded later. And he never went back. But Suzuki certainly did. And Hailwood won on their bike. Backed by the full Suzuki Grand Prix works team who had seen Sheene's island debut and were only too keen to present Hailwood with a great chance for a finale to remember, a proven world-beater bike, and to stamp their identity on the most problematical track in motorcycle racing.

The Italian pin-up boy, Giacomo Agostini, twelve times world champion, roared home to ten TT triumphs in sixteen attempts on the unbeatable and formidably quick and reliable MV Agusta, and would have more than likely continued to race on there but for his despair at the unfortunate death of his long-term best pal Gilberto Parlotti, the ninety-ninth competitor to die.

The thirty-two-year-old Italian, the 125cc world championship leader, was killed when he lost control and his two-stroke Morbidelli twin swerved off at 100 mph and ploughed into a series of concrete pillars lining the rain-drenched circuit at the Verandah, on his second lap as he led the race on his debut by 18 seconds.

Ago was devastated. He had taken time off from his own preparations to drive Parlotti around the circuit in his own car to point out the likely perils and danger spots – and, such was his upset, he thought seriously about not competing in the follow-up Senior TT. He tearfully declared: 'The TT is too dangerous. There are far too many bad places. One crash, one wrong move and – phut, you are dead or badly hurt. I promise I will never race there again.' And he never did. For Ago the TT died with Parlotti.

My fascination with road racing on confrontational tracks

like the TT, the superfast North West 200 in Northern Ireland and around Macau's awesome and tight 3.8-mile street circuit, brushing the walls with my shoulder, is overwhelming, and those tracks give me a buzz like no other.

The lure of the TT has a universal reach, with admirers of the event's spectacular races unashamedly eager to praise it and its legendary competitors as a showcase for dash and daring on the outer edges of courage and expertise.

The list of mainstream celebrities who only too readily offer their appreciation and express their admiration for the races is a telling reflection of the appeal of the TT to all manner of people, and it echoes the opinions of millions more attenders and visitors who are not privileged to have their views aired in public.

Ahead of the 2016 TT the likes of F1 drivers, MotoGP aces, sportsmen, and even film and rock stars, all onetime guests, were only too pleased to be asked by the programme planners for their summing-up and memories of the races.

I am grateful to Simon Crellin, the TT press and publicity officer, for letting me in on the names, which range from Hollywood megastar and action man Clint Eastwood, a keen biker, who watched in the 1970s from the Waterworks, to F1 legend and three times world champion Jackie Stewart, knighted for his achievements on four wheels but an open admirer of us two-wheeled guys.

The Scot was the F1 crown holder in 1969, 1971 and 1973 and winner of twenty-seven F1 races, when the mortality rate in his chosen profession was as scary as can be and ballsy driving, wheel-to-wheel, was paramount.

He stood on the Glencrutchery Road start line amid all the hustle and bustle and racket that precedes the waving off of the keyed-up entrants facing the first lap of 37¾ miles.

'This is man's country,' I am told is what he said as he watched us roar away down awesome Bray Hill at 190 mph in the 2012 TT, a comeback race I thought I was going to have to miss after awkwardly twisting my leg while riding an off-road bike pre-season. But that's another story to come . . .

Jackie said he had been blown away by the courage and skill of TT riders after watching the documentary movie *TT3D: Closer to the Edge* in 2011 and decided he had to pay a visit to see for himself just what a spectacle the race is.

As the programme noted, speaking at the premiere of the film, Jackie enthused: 'I have always admired the TT riders. I think they've got more courage and more skills than almost any sport that I know of. And it is by far the most difficult track to do properly. I just take my hat off to them all. In a Formula One car you've got things around you as protection – but on a bike you are very exposed and when you are racing around the Isle of Man, doing the speeds that these guys do, that takes courage – that takes a *lot* of courage. And I mean a *LOT*!'

The programme also featured Valentino Rossi, the Italian Motorcycle Grand Prix champion nine times on a 125cc in 1997, 250cc in 1999, 500cc in 2001, MotoGP in 2002–2005 and 2008–2009 – and, it is said, arguably the greatest and most famous motorcycle racer of all time.

According to the programme, 'Valentino not only turned up to watch the TT in 2009 he did a lap of honour on a Yamaha R1 and he said, "I am fascinated by all motorsport and the Isle of Man is a destination and a race I have always wanted to experience for a very long time. Always the MotoGP schedule is very busy around this time of the year but this year the TT has moved dates a little and there is a week's gap between Mugello and Catalunya so now at least I have the opportunity to make the visit."

'After his lap on the road-going Yamaha R1 Rossi was even more respectful, saying "It impressed me a lot because I know that it is dangerous and also very fast. I don't expect a road like this to be a track and it is unbelievable to be going flat-out around it on a Superbike. You need to have two great big balls! To be flat-out you need a lot of bravery and technique. For the riders who do this race it is like a battle. It is different to MotoGP, very impressive, it is very dangerous and you dare not make a mistake."'

His impression was shared by ex-F1 driver and Le Mans ace Mark Webber, a Grand Prix winner nine times, and World Endurance champion in 2015. No stranger to a career on the very edge, the Australian ace, keenly hooked on the event, visited the TT five times, in 2008, 2012, 2013, 2014 and 2015. And his promise to himself is that he will maintain his enthusiasm for the Manx campaign and keep on making the trip as long as it does not clash with his own race responsibilities.

'It really is man and machine in the most courageous scenario imaginable,' said Webber. 'You feel the bikes fly past you and the feeling you get from that sensation is incredible. It's completely raw and makes you look on in total admiration. One second it is peaceful and quiet and the next the electrifying roar of a bike at 200 mph cuts right through you to the core and leaves an unforgettable impression. That's why Formula One guys like Sebastian Vettel and Jenson Button, real bike race fans, have all said they want to have a go.'

His great pal is my big rival and TT torment John McGuinness. 'The first year I visited I was a guest of John McGuinness. He got us a great viewing spot just before the riders drop into the famous compression at Bray Hill. I was standing there with my dad and we were both gobsmacked by the courage on show. In fact, it was emotional to see riders on a missile of a bike hurtling around a normal road used by traffic, cars, lorries and buses, every day when the race is not on. My dad has seen a lot of racing action over the years and so have I, both as competitor and spectator, but it was definitely the biggest thing the both of us have ever seen. A gigantic thrill. It is a full-on experience and something I will never forget for the rest of my life.'

Another motorcycle racer and MotoGP world champion, Jorge Lorenzo, paid a visit in 2010 and recalls: 'What an amazing experience. I did a lap on a Yamaha R1 road bike and now I understand why people enjoy the sensation of racing at the TT. I only did one lap and I would definitely like some more practice around the circuit. I was able to do a few wheelies and wave a lot to what was a fantastic crowd of so many fans. I had read all about the TT in magazines and had seen it on television but nothing can prepare you for the real experience. And I was only playing about. I didn't have to try to be a winner. But wow . . .'

Bike heroes galore have attended to watch and wonder at the immensity of the challenge that confronts those who face up to the Mountain Circuit's formidable obstacles. Mick Doohan, Kevin Schwantz, Loris Capirossi, Jonathan Rea, John Hopkins, Neil Hodgson, Colin Edwards – the 'Texas Tornado' – Colin Crutchlow, Bradley Smith and Randy Mamola, all two-wheeled stars in world-title chasing on Grand Prix circuits, have been transfixed trackside. Nigel Mansell, too, the daredevil and fearless world F1 champion and for a long time a resident on the island, is a declared fan. He said: 'Going about my business every day on those roads gave me an insight into what the TT guys have to do at 200 miles an hour to be a winner. I can't begin to explain my admiration for their ability and attitude.'

That is, indeed, a tribute. Not bad coming from a man who had known no fear when he was dicing wheel-to-wheel, week after week, with some scary drivers at the same speed we now get to around the island.

And the fan base doesn't stop there. Eric Bana, the Hollywood actor and star of *Hulk* and *Star Trek*, paid a visit in 2012 to support fellow Aussie Cameron Donald – and, years on, he can't stop talking about the experience. 'I had wanted for years to make the trip to the TT because a few mates of mine had managed to do it and they had driven me mad with jealousy with their stories and descriptions of the races and riders and the whole fantastic set-up in an atmosphere like no other. I was in London shooting a film and, thanks to the Queen and a UK bank holiday to celebrate her Diamond Jubilee, I managed to get few days off. I just jumped on the first flight I could catch to get there as soon as I could. And in no time at all I was revelling in the unbelievable . . . sitting in someone's front garden on Bray Hill. When the first three bikes came through I was just speechless. I'd never seen anything like it.'

International cricketer Darren Gough, former Yorkshire skipper and one of England's most successful wicket-takers, visited in 2013. And he recalls: 'I have always been a fan of watching motorbike racing – but it had always been British Superbikes, World Superbikes and MotoGP. To go to the TT was amazing. And I take my hat off to all those guys who race there. It is just pure skill and guts.'

I'll wrap up this list of celebrity spectators by quoting offbeat Ross Noble, one of the Britain's best-loved comedians and voted one of the top ten greatest stand-up comics of all time.

He was hell-bent on seeing the TT and he somehow managed to mix business with the pleasure of getting to the island by taking his stage act to Douglas, performing at the Villa Marina. He had been fired up to go after doing a lap on a bike in 2009. And as soon as he could he was back. He said, somewhat bizarrely: 'I always enjoyed going past the Wildlife Park at Quarry Bends. Then I have a thought: with that giant otter standing just outside the park at the side of the road I wonder what the racers think as they fly past at 150 mph and see it staring at them.'

CHAPTER 2

ABILITY OVER ADVERSITY

I find it fascinating, but at the same time difficult to believe, that people are referring to me when I read or hear some of the generously laudatory remarks mentioning my name and praising my achievements. And I have to pinch myself to make sure I'm not dreaming. Perhaps I can just say that smug self-satisfaction and ego-tripping are not a part of my character. Far from it. Neither do I dwell on, or look for sympathy for, the mishaps like the awful 2010 Silverstone accident in 2010, when I crashed and was run over, and so badly injured that the incident could have spelt the end of my career. I will return to that nightmarish episode, a crucial career-threatening setback, a bit later on, even though it means reliving my own vivid and agonising memories.

It is, however, pinpointed by Paul Butler, the well-respected former head of MotoGP, whom I first met when I rode in the Macau Grand Prix in 2005, my rookie year, and he was officiating at the formidable Far East street race. I finished tenth overall but second in the Supersport class, a race that is now for 1,000cc bikes.

Paul, who started his motorcycle race career as the competitions manager for Dunlop Tyres in 1969, and later moved to Yamaha Racing, based in Amsterdam, has seen in close-up all the true greats over the decades, and has been typically generous in his assessment of my ability and attitude. 'One characteristic that all champions share,' he said, 'is a steely, unswerving focus and determination to do whatever it takes to be a winner.

'Most people who meet Hutchy away from the track are first impressed by his softly spoken Yorkshire accent and his youthful good looks. And they are amazed when they find out he is the only motorcycle racer to have won five Isle of Man TT races in one week. That most impressive feat, truly memorable, was achieved in 2010 followed just three months later by his dreadful crash at Silverstone that could have ended all his dreams of a future in motorcycle racing at the very top level. I saw the massive extent of damage to his left leg when he appeared, barely able to walk, in London at the premiere of the race movie *Closer to the Edge*.

'It was difficult to imagine he could fully recover enough to race again – and the next time I met him was when he had bravely and successfully battled his problems and was back in Macau in November 2013, riding Shaun Muir's Milwaukee Yamaha with the gear shift switched to the right side and modified to ease mobility problems with his left lower leg. Before his Silverstone smash he raced Macau four more times and finished third twice.

'I didn't get to know Ian much better during the days leading up to the race when he made his Macau comeback after his terrible accident since, typical of his attitude, he was rarely seen by anybody outside his immediate team, because his first priority, leading up to the opening practice session, was to seek out the local gym and then spend just about every waking hour working out like a committed Olympian to fix and strengthen his wounded body.

'Parallels can be drawn between Hutchy and other heroic victims of worrying life-and-career-threatening crashes, like former 500cc world champion Barry Sheene, another faller left with really serious injuries in scary circumstances at Silverstone, and the Aussie multi-champ ace Mick Doohan, who steadfastly spurned attempts to amputate his lower leg. They both summoned up the courage to fight through the intense pain barrier to achieve the Holy Grail of a return to the sport they loved. As winners all over again.'

Paul, who recalls my return to Macau in 2013 in remarkable detail, goes on: 'Hutchy's first appearance on the new Milwaukee Yamaha was in Thursday morning's free practice session. The early-morning session is an acclimatisation for the riders to a circuit that only a couple of hours before had buses, heavy trucks and all manner of vehicles trekking on it and leaving their deposits. Hutchy, I remember, completed fifteen laps and his best time ranked him fifth behind Michael Rutter, Jimmy Storrar, Horst Saiger and John McGuinness.

'The next session, Qualifying 1, started at 3.50 p.m. the same day. It followed on a mass of circuit activity with Formula 3, GT and World Touring cars adding to the uncertainty and dirtiness of the track, but the overall adhesion was improved by the streams of rubber put down by the four-wheelers.

'Ian's seventeen laps moved him up to fourth fastest just 2.2 seconds adrift of Rutter and behind McGuinness and Martin Jessop. After a de-brief with his team it was back to the gym for yet another tough work-out to ready himself for final qualifying at 7.30 a.m. on Friday morning.

'I was amazed at Hutchy's admirable resilience and resolve and his formidable unstinting effort to ensure that his physical fitness level could cope with the demands he was clearly determined to put it under. And worthily it paid off. Qualifying 2 saw his eleven laps of gutsy, dauntless riding promote him to pole position for Saturday's big race with a quickest lap of 2.25.568, averaging a very impressive 94 mph, just in front of Rutter, a Macau Grand Prix winner eight times, and nearly two seconds ahead of third-placed John McGuinness, two exceptional road race legends.

'The scene was the forty-seventh staging of the Macau Grand Prix, an invitation race for thirty-two riders based on past performances in classic road races like the Isle of Man TT, the North West 200 in Northern Ireland, and the Ulster Grand Prix, around the very physically demanding 3.8 mile Guia circuit, with its nineteen corners and only seven metres wide in some sections, and it was clear to me that Hutchy was really up for it and had the capability to equal his ambition.

'The show started at 3.34 p.m. in dry conditions, 23 degrees centigrade, but Hutchy's start, maybe because of a tall first gear in his Yamaha, was not the best, not what I imagine he really expected. But in real hell-bent and fearless style, inside two laps he forced his way past McGuinness and Gary Johnson before mounting his attack on race leader Michael Rutter, the most successful Macau achiever of all time and looking for a record ninth crown, on the fourth lap, passing him, and pulling out a two-second lead. That was the gap he maintained until the race was red flagged and cut short due to an incident on the twelfth lap. Rutter finished second, Johnson was third with McGuinness fourth and Jimmy Storrar fifth

'Hutchy's victory, a triumph of ability over adversity, was a vivid testimony to his resolve, grit and determination and his dogged refusal to kowtow to the danger that his racing career could have been over and done with three years . . . and a lot of surgery . . . earlier. No wonder that, after the finish, his rivals lined up to congratulate one very tearful and emotional winner.

'Macau is a vibrant and buzzing place, often described with some justification as the Las Vegas of the Orient. It is a haven of fun and frolic, and the night after Hutchy's splendid win it lived up to its raucous reputation. The emotion surrounding his truly great win was reflected in the respect and delight shown by his fellow riders, all well beaten, who celebrated in just about the best party I have ever been to out there, fuelled by Monster Energy with a little help from Grey Goose. That night, in the Lion Bar of the MGM Grand Hotel and Casino, the team principals from Milwaukee Yamaha and SMT Honda, Rutter's team, along with Ian's great mates Shaun Muir and Robin Croft and a whole gang of riders and officials, went flat out to hail one of the most memorable and extra-specially remarkable comeback victories in the history of motorcycle racing.'

When I read Paul's assessment of my win against all those top-class road racers I can scarcely believe that this had all happened to me. To look back now and re-run that spell in my mind's eye is like looking in on an action replay of a dream come true. But it was achieved only through hard work. Every day. And never for a split second with the remotest thought of ever relaxing from the effort and strain, and much less of giving up.

I had about ten plans in mind for the race, but the main one was to go for it and get in front as early as I could. I would have preferred to have made it to the chequered flag rather than winning with the race being stopped. That would have been a bit more special – but, importantly, we got the victory and it was the perfect way to thank everybody in the team who had stood by me with such confidence and loyalty.

I remember thinking: 'That is one of the most special wins I have ever had with all that has hit me and plunged my job in danger over the last three years. Hopefully we can now put everything that happened to me with my leg behind us and take up where we left off three years ago.'

That magic in Macau . . . around Fisherman's Bend, up the San Francisco and Faraway Hills, through Maternity Bend, risking it through the Solitude Esses . . . was a kick-start to the second phase, another telling and fruitful episode in my career. But, first, let's get back to the beginning . . .

CHAPTER 3

BEGINNINGS

How did I get started as a motorcycle racer, more especially with a positive leaning towards road racing in preference to short-circuit competition?

Well, unlike most motorcycle racers I didn't start off with motorcycles as a kid. I'm told by my parents that if I ever heard or saw a motorbike going past I used to jump out of my pram to watch it. I always used to ask if I could have a motorbike, or even ride one. But my Dad was in the furniture business and I have two sisters, so my mum was at home with the kids most of the time and I just never had motorbikes as a kid. I just had the usual things, pushbikes and normal things that kids have. I went to a private school from the ages of about six to ten, and that was the first time I came across a motorbike. I had a friend called Tom

Walton, whose dad actually follows me now. (He comes to a lot of racing. He came up to my car one day and I hadn't seen him for probably twenty years.) He had a motorbike, and it was the first one I ever sat on. It was a Yamaha TY80 and neither he nor Tom were much bothered about it, but every time I went to their house I just wanted to get this bike out of their garage. That was my first go on one, and we didn't really do anything crazy on it or get much time on it on big land, or anything like that.

He lived next to a golf course, and I think we got the bike out there. Tom's dad also had a big industrial unit and we rode the Yamaha round that a bit, but otherwise that was that. Then, aged ten, I wasn't really clever enough to go on to another private school, I don't think, but that was the next step: you went to older private school from then on and obviously its a lot of money to go to those places, and we moved house as well. But there was a good local school, Bingley Grammar School, so I ended up there. I actually attended a middle school for one year in between because the years were out a little, before going on to grammar school. At the middle school I made friends with a boy called Martin Crosswaite who was British Youth Trials Champion, and it was as though trials riding was almost a profession for him at that age, around fifteen years old. He lived just up the road from us and his parents had a lovely big house and loads of land, perfect for trials riding. I used to rush home from school and run up the snickets to his house and watch him – he was that good as a trials rider. That really got me hooked, and I begged to have a go at it. I was due to go on holiday with my family about a week later and I pleaded with him to let me have a go on his bike. He finally gave way and let me. And it ended in disaster. I used too much front brake on the grass, locked the wheel and fell off the bike. Unfortunately, something stuck in my knee and punctured an artery so I ended up in hospital and came home with my leg in a half cast, walking on crutches just a week or so before going on holiday.

That didn't do me any favours with my parents as far as motorbikes were concerned. I was fourteen or fifteen at the time. They never had liked motorbikes so that was probably one of the worst things that could have happened. However, they saw that I was mad keen, and I must have become so much of a pest they decided they had better get me a trials bike before I reached the age of seventeen and wanted a road bike. I got a Yamaha TY175 then and started doing some trials, and my dad got a TY250 and started coming, even though he was never into bikes. There was a local quarry called the Flappet that any random person with a motorbike used to go to on a Sunday and so we used to go up there. We must have stood out like sore thumbs because we each had a battered full-face helmet with no visor, for we had no idea what you were supposed to wear; I think my dad had wellies on and corduroy trousers. But that was it so far as I was concerned, and I never turned back from that fun time on two wheels. I went a step further when I earned an apprenticeship at Colin Appleyard's motorcycle business in Keighley.

Colin (who sadly died in 2015) was a really well-known bike fanatic and supporter, and I think, as far as I can recall, that I got the job through school. They asked me what I would like to do and I said I want to be a motorcycle mechanic, and they got me into Colin Appleyard's for my work experience. My week's work experience went well, and I think they must have liked me because I got a Saturday job with them and worked every Saturday up until leaving school at sixteen, when I started my apprenticeship there full time. I was on a block release (which allows employees to take stated periods off work in order to attend an educational course) and went to Bridlington College for two weeks at a time.

I had never seen any bike racing or anything like it, so there was no particular urge to take up racing at that time, it was simply a case of riding bikes. Full stop. I took my car test really quickly within two or three weeks or turning seventeen and passed it, but my bike test was an absolute nightmare. The government were in the process of changing the rules about how old a rider had to be to take the bike test, so if I didn't take it now I would have to wait until I was twenty-one once the new rules came into play. I failed the first test I took for riding over-cautiously, I think it was, and my instructor couldn't believe it. In fact, I had the craziest instructor – he had a very large and powerful bike and during lessons he would ride around on that while I struggled to keep up with him. It was mad. I was more nervous of going too fast in the test because of the way I had been riding around with him, so in the event I ended up being too cautious. But then, in my second test, I did the opposite, and was failed for that. So I booked a third test, and on the way there a school kid suddenly ran out into the road and got stuck between traffic going one way and traffic going the other and me coming down the middle. I clipped his foot and slid off. Luckily, I was okay, but I got to the test centre with broken indicators and they wouldn't allow me take the test. By then it was the last week before Christmas, and I think it was on the 20 or 21 December that the test centres were closing for the holiday, and wouldn't reopen until the new year. But on 1 January the new rules came into force, meaning you would have to be twenty-one to take your bike test . . . So I got my mum to ring up every single test centre in the country and find me somewhere to take my test before 1 January. Eventually I got in for one at Doncaster before Christmas. I didn't have a clue where Doncaster was or anything, but we had a trailer for the trials bikes, and I had a 125 that Appleyard's had lent me to take my test on. At first they had loaned me a Yamaha DT125. I had failed two previous tests on it and been knocked off it on my way to the third, and I just said I think the test people think I am going to be too much of a rebel to be a safe and competent motorcyclist.

There I was, a seventeen-year-old with a Colin Appleyard's jacket and all that, and they swapped the damaged Yamaha for a Suzuki GN125 for me and I put it on the trailer behind the car and drove down to Doncaster. I had no idea of any of the roads in the city – never been there, never had a lesson there. I parked in a Morrison's car park and put on a wax jacket with a big reflective yellow stripe, and wax overtrousers, and made myself look as safe and as numpty as possible. It was December, so it was cold. I found the test centre and set out on my test. There was one road we came up to, it was big and it went over a main road to a junction with another main road, and if the examiner didn't say turn left or right then you were meant go straight over. Fair enough. But in the event he didn't say anything and I had missed that at the junction you were only permitted to go straight or turn left. So I looked over my shoulder, did the checks and indicated to turn left, thinking there is no way I can go straight ahead: there are four lanes of traffic going across, it looks like a massive road, I must have missed a sign saying you can only turn left. So stopped at the lights and as soon as they changed and I came to the crest I was able to see that I could have gone straight on, in fact. My heart just sank and I thought, That's it, I'm not passing my test. I carried on with my left turn, went through the rest of my test feeling gutted, got back to the test centre . . . and the examiner passed me, despite my clanger.

When he told me I'd passed he said I looked surprised. I

said, well yes, I thought I had gone the wrong way. He said that I had, but I had done everything else right, I had done all my checks and had indicated as necessary and safely: 'So I can't fail you for going the wrong way,' he added. That was it. If it hadn't happened that day I don't think that I would ever have raced a bike. It would have been another four years before I could even have ridden a road bike.

It was lucky, but in a sense, this was Fate playing her hand. Missing or failing my test might have put me off biking for ever. The absolute trigger point for my interest in bikes had been meeting Martin at school – that was where I basically rooted it. I wanted to follow him, be around him. It really was as simple as that, because people need a trigger point and this was mine.

He or his parents actually own a local pub. He does some motorcycle stunt shows on his trials bike, but he is married with a kid now, like most of my friends, so I don't see much of him. But when I opened my own motorcycle-repair business in 2003 I had a unit right next to his, so I worked with him pretty much every day. I had a workshop doing my own mechanical repairs and he was in the unit next door importing trials bikes and selling clothing and accessories – he was the UK importer for a lot of things. So from 2003 to 2006 Martin and I worked out of the same unit, although since I went down the racing route I have seen much less of him.

Because I never followed bike racing of any sort as a child

and in my early teens I never had anyone to follow or to suggest that that was what I wanted to do. After passing my test I was still working at Appleyard's, and there was a group of young lads who used to come in, and I remember seeing them out the back with their bikes. One had a Suzuki RGV250, one had a Honda CBR400 and one had a Kawasaki ZXR400 and I just thought they all looked very cool, and like they were having a real good time. It all just looked awesome to me. Then, once I had finished my apprenticeship with Appleyard's I moved from there to work at Allan Jefferies's bike business. Tony, a great TT rider in his heyday, was sadly left in a wheelchair after being badly and permanently damaged in a crash. It didn't stop him continuing with his family business and giving it all his concentration, however.

At Appleyard's there was a guy called Lee Morton who had been the apprentice before me, and I think he was like mid-twenties by the time I finished my apprenticeship. He was always known as 'the apprentice' even at that age, and I remember thinking I don't want to be that, I want to be recognised as a fully fledged mechanic. So I moved to Jefferies and built up a whole new set of friends and eager bike-racing enthusiasts. At a local pub I got to meet the gang of lads that used to come into Appleyard's. I became really good friends with them, and on the strength of that I bought a Yamaha TZR250. At the time I didn't have a clue how good or how trick the bike was.

How did I afford it? The answer is that I got it on finance. The bike came in as a part-exchange at Jefferies and I just saw it and loved it, immediately thinking, What can I do to get this bike? At Jefferies they worked out a finance package for me. At the time the TZR250 was a really trick bike, although I didn't know much about it; it and its bigger brother, the TZR350, both twin-cylinder 2-strokes, had taken the bike world by storm on their introduction in 1986, and they stayed in production for ten years. I just liked the look of it more than anything. So I bought it and started going out with these lads. And they knew another group who were older, a lot of guys in their late thirties and early forties. I was still seventeen then. My friends were mostly twenty or twenty-one, about three years older. So I started going out with all of these and very quickly began to learn how to ride fast, because they had been doing it for quite a while. I was just crazy on this bike. We used to ride for miles on a Wednesday, and on Sundays we would travel up to Coniston and the Lake District, getting up at 7 a.m. on Sunday mornings and setting off before most people were awake. We had some amazing times. It was fantastic to go riding road bikes around places like that. The freedom, the open air and open roads, were a total joy. Today the roads are so busy that you couldn't even explain to anyone how good it was to do that.

We didn't use the roads as a racetrack, but there was definitely a competitive edge to our riding. Obviously we all wanted to be the best, and it didn't take me very long before I was the fastest of the group. I then moved on to a Kawasaki ZXR400 and my friends all moved on to bigger bikes as well – mainly Honda Fireblades and Kawasaki ZX7s. So, aged nineteen, I bought a Fireblade, although when I look back now I don't know how it happened. I had no money, I was working as a bike mechanic for a couple of hundred pounds a week but I still lived at home, and I had this Fireblade!

In the meantime I had gone through quite a few cars as well, so it was clear that I was no good at keeping the things on the road. I started off by crashing my mum's car. I had been at Carnaby College in East Yorkshire for about a year, studying for my apprenticeship, and as my parents were going on holiday I asked if I could I take mum's car – I had been getting the train up until then. The lads that were at the college with me were a bit of a mixed age group. We used to stop in a B&B, probably six or eight of us together, and it was a great time. When I went back with my mum's car, no one else had one. We would go into college every day and then mess around. The college was right on the airfield where the racetrack used to be, so one lunchtime we came back from Bridlington and went onto the airfield to risk some handbrake turns and stuff. I couldn't do an effective handbrake spin in the car – it was a Fiat Panda, and with five lads in it, it was too heavy for the handbrake to work – so we were doing reverse turns: flat out in reverse, full steering wheel and swinging the front round. On the fourth attempt the car rolled over onto its roof. We were all bounced around and a bit shaken, but, luckily nobody was hurt so we all got out and dragged the car off its roof and set it right way up. I had an engine jack at the college, and with that I jacked the roof back out so I could get another windscreen in, drove it home to a guy I knew, Ian, who ran Great Northern Cars at the bottom of the road down from Colin Appleyard's. I had to beg him because I was only on £30 per week, plus my Saturday money, and I promised to pay him £10 per week for as long as it took to fix the car. So he accepted my offer and, thankfully, did a great job in repairing it. I was supposed to take it back home during the weekend in the middle of term, but obviously I couldn't come back from college because Ian hadn't finished and I had no transport. But the following week I came home and he put in a lot of time and effort rushing to get it all finished and cleaned out inside so that I could take it home in pristine nick. He did such an expert job that my mum never even noticed.

I think Ian recently met up with my parents. He'd had a few beers and let the secret out when he mentioned repairing the Fiat to my mum and dad. I'd have kept my mouth shut!

Unfortunately, the car took another hit a couple of months later when I crashed it into a telegraph pole and all the filler came out of the roof. I thought, I am going to get caught for the last one now, because the insurance company is going to see where the filler has come out of the roof. I waited for the post to see whether they were going to pay out for the car, but my parents did get paid so they still never knew about the first crash. But then I had a few crashes in my own car. I bought a Peugeot 205 GTi, and on one occasion I lost the back end and crashed into a wall at speed.

It was basically my instinct to go for it either on a bike or driving a car. It just seemed second nature to me to want to go quick. Obviously, when I look back now and drive cars fast I realise how little I knew back then. At that age you don't know when and where to be slow and when to be fast. You think every corner can be taken at the same speed. Wrong!

I did not have any real heroes – until Dave Jefferies, Tony's son, came into my life. When I went to work at Jefferies I got to meet Dave, for he was always in and out of the place. I didn't know him well when I first worked there, but obviously I had seen him around. I would go in to work on a Monday morning and his great big fifth-wheel camper would be in the car park because he couldn't get it up the drive where they lived. So his American pick-up and his camper would be parked the full length of the car park, and then come 10 or 11 o'clock he would come strolling out of the camper and drive it down to where he stored it. Then he would come back down in a big truck or a Mitsubishi Evo or whatever – he had so many toys. He would appear at work in something different every hour of the day, and come bouncing through the workshop. To me, a curious and completely fascinated onlooker, his life looked absolutely perfect. I just loved everything about what he was doing, about his whole lifestyle.

So I started to follow him as a racer, for he was campaigning a Triumph at the time. Obviously I didn't understand enough about the sport to realise or appreciate the level he was at. But I started watching him avidly. He was a regular winner and that was my introduction to following anyone racing. His tragically cruel death later hit me really hard, and made me only too aware of just how dangerous bike racing can be, even for the greatest and safest riders. Dave, a TT winner nine times and the first competitor to lap the island course at 125 mph, was killed during practice for the 2003 TT. At Crosby he ran into a patch of oil on the track while doing 160 mph and smashed head on into a wall. He was killed instantly. Awful . . . and a dreadful loss to the sport.

But to return to my initiation as a committed follower of the sport with a constant hunger either to be on my bike or trackside, watching with genuine admiration all those guys going for it flat-out, shoulder-to-shoulder.

A couple of lads in the group that I knocked about with on Sundays were into the World Superbikes and one of them, Matthew Dobbins, used to wear a James Whitham helmet. He had pictures of James and the great Carl Fogarty on his walls at home, and he loved watching the World Superbikes races. So we started to go and watch events at Donington

Park, camping out at the tent site. I think for the MotoGP we never actually watched the race; instead we'd do all the lunatic stuff in the campsite and come home on Sunday and watch on TV what we had not bothered to watch live at the track. It was weird. I watched racing, but it wasn't like a bug where I just had to be doing it. I loved going to the tracks and doing what we were doing, but that was it. We used to buy old cars from scrapyards just to take down to the Superbike races for the campsite, rally them around the place and burn them at the end of the day. Or we would take Honda C90s or scooters and mess about on them. The campsite was awesome, a fantastic atmosphere with all sorts of stuff going on all day and all night. We used to have so much fun, it was just great to be there. We never caused any trouble, but obviously some stuff looks reckless, although we never really did anything that naughty.

When you are absorbed in some activity to that level, with an increasing interest, and you can see the way you want to go, you begin to think, This is what I want to do for a living. In my case, all my instincts were to be daring, to be right on the edge and to go fast and then faster, to compete, to be the fastest, the best in my group. Or any other . . .

Going back to when I got the TZR, the group of lads that I rode with used to go to the Isle of Man every year to watch the TT. Inevitably, I opted to go with them one year, and that was my first insight into the race, in 1997. We all caught the ferry to the island at Heysham, in Lancashire, having hung around at the ferry port for twenty-four hours, waiting to get aboard. All our talk was about the Isle of Man and the events we were so keyed up to watch. Within about two hours of getting off the ferry at Douglas I had flipped a wheelie on my TZR. I tried to do what everybody on a bike was doing pretty much everywhere, and obviously a 250cc TZR with me on it lugging a massive rucksack on my back is not really meant for doing wheelies everywhere. Other riders had hot-stuff Fireblades and similar mega-bikes. So it was carnage before we had even started. I had worked hard to convince my parents to let me go. I was seventeen, but they weren't keen on me going to the TT on a bike. Full stop. They didn't know much about it, but they knew it was dangerous. So having crashed so soon after arriving on the island wasn't ideal.

We got off the ferry, went and had some breakfast then we set out to look for the the place where we were staying. And I crashed. Not on the course, obviously, not racing, just popping a wheelie. So inside a couple of hours on the island, I was off. We were stopping in a homestay this time, and I needed to get my bike fixed. I had to put an inner tube in the back wheel because the rim had cracked (the tyre was tubeless), and we went up to the paddock and got some bits off Dennis Trollope, whose team were racing TZRs back then. Luckily they had all the bits I needed.

I can't remember if we were there for five days or a week, but we used to get up every day and ride around and get stuck in with the the Mad Sunday masses riding over the Mountain circuit. We used to go up to the Mountain and then back through Laxey because we weren't that interested in doing a full lap. We just wanted to go over the Mountain. Then we would find somewhere to watch all the others giving it a go. I have some great pictures of us sitting on trackside bankings, shirts off, sun out – we used to get terribly, painfully sunburnt but we didn't care. It was just brilliant going out and watching, although at that time I never sat there thinking, I want to do this for a living.

It was good that Dave Jefferies was in the races then. He had started doing the TT, and so from a really early stage in his career we were following him at a time when no one had really heard of him. Especially in 1999, when we were on the island and somebody in the crowd asked us who we were there to support and we all chanted 'Dave Jefferies' – and they were like, 'Do you know him?' He went on to win three races that year so we were chuffed to bits.

We went to the TT again in 1998, a year after my first visit, and as near as I can recall I think I went for about five years on the trot. We used to do all the crazy stuff on the Promenade in Douglas. We loved joining in with all the other bikers for a night show, getting the bikes out and doing wheelies and burn-outs. The whole atmosphere was amazing, like nothing I have ever experienced anywhere. Here were 40,000 or 50,000 people on the island just for the fun, the spectacle of the races and the excitement of being part of what was, and is, a unique scene. It was incredible to be involved in it: everyone wanted to be a racer, or at least to be part of the atmosphere. There was no fighting, no fall-outs or ill-feeling, no bad times at all – only friendly, albeit competitive, showdowns on two wheels or, more often, just one.

The Promenade was the best bit. In those days I was more into stunt riding than racing, and I loved watching other riders' antics and just wanted to be one of them. I would go off practising and climb on my tank and do sat-on-the-tank wheelies. Even though I was a mechanic I never sussed out exactly how other riders could do some of the things they could do. Now I know that they would fit much larger rear sprockets to lower the gearing. I would see them doing circle wheelies at just a few miles per hour, and would think, My Fireblade won't do that unless I am doing 40mph, so how does that work? Now I know. I loved all the stunts that drew us into returning year after year, and doing all the mad stuff on the Promenade in front of so many like-minded people. Only in the first year I went did we stay in proper accommodation; from then on we used to keep bikes in a van, put some mattresses in, sleep on Douglas prom and then bring the bikes outside onto the Promenade for some show-off spells.

It is curious to look back and remember, for it is a massive leap from those days to now. There you were, sleeping in a van and enjoying life and the atmosphere at the back end of the TT because you couldn't afford to stay in hotels . . .

if you could get into the hotels anyway. They were always full and paid up long before the visitors' annual arrivals. I preferred to sleep in a van, and play on the bike. Then I made history by winning *five* races in a week – and my whole TT life changed. For the better. No wonder, because I won something like £80,000 in prize money. Ironically, I was riding for long-time sponsor and TT backer Clive Padgett for free at the time.

Today the prize money is going down. Before I started it was £22,000 for the Superbike or the Senior and now it is £18,000. It was £20,000 when I first won them. I don't understand how it is that the TT is getting better than ever, and yet thirty years ago you got 4 grand more for winning each of those races.

But let me go back to how and why I developed the first pangs of wanting to move on and become a real racer.

The motivation came from the group I rode with, basically. With the roads getting increasingly busy, and us riding more and more like racers on them, we decided that we would take part in some track days at a time when track days were still very new. It was not like nowadays, when they are relatively common. So three or four of us, a main group consisting of Steve, Matt, my very best friend Craig Atkinson, and me all went and did a couple of track days at Cadwell Park. I really loved doing that, but we were on our road bikes – so the next idea was, Why don't we start racing on proper stuff? In the meantime, I left Jefferies to go and work for Hobbsport

Racing, a race-engine tuner. As a result of my working there I started to learn a lot about engine building and tuning, and ended up the main engine builder there. Obviously race bikes were coming in every day, and by working on them I got to know a lot more about them. So among our group I suggested that we should just get some cheap 600cc race bikes and go and do some cup racing. So Matt, Craig and I – Steve wasn't really into it. I don't know if he was that interested start with, and he wasn't as good as us three – each got a 600 race bike through somebody Mark, the boss at Hobbsport, knew. Then we were given a caravan, a big 17-footer. It was always a laughing stock as it was a proper skip of a thing, but Craig I went and picked it up and gave it a lick of paint, cleaned it out a bit, put a new carpet in it, and that was it. Three of us setting up, and we borrowed the Hobbsport team van, a Daf Sherpa, to tow the caravan with the bikes in it. It was one of the ones that Daf produced with V8 engines for ambulances and police riot vans. Mark, the boss, had worked for Daf so he got an engine and put it into his van, and back then a V8 Sherpa was a serious bit of kit. It used to guzzle fuel and we never had any money, so it was a bit of a waste going round club racing with it. We put a side pipe exhaust on it – in fact, I think it was the exhaust off a Peugeot GTi 1.9 that I had crashed. There was nothing much left of the car so the exhaust came off that and went onto the van. And that was our transport for our club racing beginnings.

The first event I ever raced in was at Mallory Park. I

didn't know much about club racing, and had never been to any of the races. We were put into two groups, A and B, because there were so many riders. So I took a walk around the paddock and looked at the list of names and saw that Craig and Matt were in the A group and I was in the B group. In the paddock I had particularly noticed two bikes – one ridden by a guy called Peter Baker, a terrific rider who has dominated club racing ever since then, and the other by a guy whose name I can't recall but, again, a very talented racer. And these two were in my group, which left me thinking, 'Oh my God, I've got no chance.' The big teams with the best riders and bikes were in my group. And that was the daunting prospect that I faced for my first steps in an absolute melee. Peter Baker was on a Honda CBR600 – beautifully prepared, it was as good as anything in the British Championship. There was a bit of a commotion on the line of the first race that my mates were in – somebody flipped a wheelie and the result was chaos. Then my friend Matt came through from the third row, led the whole race and won it. His first ever race. Then came my race. I had been lapping a second a lap faster than Matt, but I finished fourth so I felt I had had a bit of a raw deal in not getting to win my first club race. I was happy because I had shown that I was pretty quick and confident. And I was certain that there was more – much more – to come from me as I progressed, building experience and know-how.

I can never remember where my first win was, but I did win races that year. We mainly raced at Cadwell, Snetterton and Croft, until I was racing as much as I could afford. I forget exactly how many races we did, but it was quite a lot.

By the end of the year, 2000, I was consistently winning races and wanted to move up. Then, the following year, a customer was having an R1 built at the shop, Hobbsport Racing. His name was Conrad Bradley and I don't know why he had spent a fortune on this bike, and it was lovely, but he then offered it to me to ride in MRO championship races. He wasn't bothered about riding it himself; in fact, I don't think he ever rode it at all. So I moved up, but my two mates, Craig and Matt, didn't seem to very keen to follow me. They were still club racing.

But I don't think I won a race all year. I had gone into it with big hopes, but I struggled right at the start because it was such a massive step up. I remember getting a third place at Snetterton when James Courtney won the race on a Ducati – a really trick Ducati – so it was good company in that class and it brought my racing on a lot. At the end of that year I moved up again into the Superstock 1000 in the British Championship. So I did one year of club racing, one year of MRO and the following year went straight into British Superstock. In fact, in 2000 and 2001 I think I was still doing some club racing and some MRO racing, a bit of everything, and then Superstock became my main interest.

But when I first switched I don't think I even qualified for my first race. There were so many Superstock riders, as there are today, sixty-odd of them, so there was a non-qualifiers' race. To be honest, 2002 is pretty vague to me because I can't remember exactly what racing I did. I was trying to do the Superstock, which was the series that Dave Jefferies was racing in. I was hanging out with him a lot more so that was a bit of a vague year, and then in 2003 I was into it again. Conrad Bradley, the guy who had lent me the R1 had got an R1000 road bike and I had converted it for racing because by then the R1 was a bit dated. Conrad helped me massively at the start of my change to road racing from the club events and up to the British Championship. But it was ages, years in fact, before I would take the big leap and turn full-time professional.

However, the Manx Grand Prix, my first major road (rather than short-circuit) race, came a long time before that, in 2003, and it came about because in 2002, when I was trying to do the British Championship and striving to be a short-circuit racer, Craig, my best friend from our group, decided to take part in that year's Manx Newcomers' race. He went out there and finished fourth in it. I was jealous then, really jealous because I knew I was better than him and he finished fourth – a great result.

The following year, 2003, we went to the island to watch David Jefferies at the TT. At the end of practice week, before we arrived, it was agreed that I would do the pit board for him during the actual races. But, tragically, he was killed in the Thursday night's practice session. I was absolutely broken by his death. I didn't know whether still to go to the island – Dave's death had made me hate the place. But we ended up going. I'll never forget it. For a start, getting to the island was a nightmare. There was low fog, the plane couldn't land at first, and it took about three attempts to get down, although it got us there in the end. A friend that I worked with at Hobbsport Racing, Tim Seed, was working as a mechanic for Bruce Anstey at the time, and he had asked me if I would be in the pits and do Bruce's wheel change. I didn't know Bruce at the time, never knew any of the big TT riders in those days, but I agreed to do the job. But then, because of the fog they cut the race down and they weren't going to do a wheel change so I never actually had to do it. But it's quite funny to think that I was going to do a wheel change for Bruce, and now I am racing against him every year.

To be honest, with Dave's death, 2003 was not a great TT for us, but on the last night we had gone out and got drunk and gone to the Casino in Douglas, and I had won £280, which just happened to be the entry fee for the Manx GP. So I put the money in an envelope and posted it through the little letterbox in the paddock for the Manx Club, and that was my entry for the 2003 Manx Grand Prix...

I remember them ringing me up and asking, 'What's this money for? And I said, 'It's my entry for the Manx.' I hadn't filled in an application form; in fact, I hadn't looked into it all. By now I had left Hobbsport Racing and opened my own business near home, so as my own boss I could take as much time off for racing as I needed. As said earlier, I rented the unit with Martin Crosswaite and did all my own work on my bikes there for the British Championship. However, I didn't have a 600 and the limit for the Manx is 750cc – all I had was an R1000. But an older guy, Rod, who used to come and help me a lot, had a 600cc Honda. I don't know how it came about, but I did a bit of begging and finally he gave way to my pleadings and lent me his bike to race in the Manx. In fact, he got involved with my plan behind the scenes and came out to the island with me.

He loved it. He had been going to the TT and the Manx GP for years, but this time he came to the island with me as my back-up mechanic. We travelled there in my little 7½-ton van, which I had started converting to be half sleeping accommodation, half workshop. And straight away we were doing well. I was third or fourth in early practice. Then by the end of the week, to my great surprise and Rod's glee– and thanks to his expert preparation – I was fastest in practice. This was a great surprise because I had never tried to learn the TT course fully, and so didn't really expect to be heading the leaderboard. I knew the Mountain section really well, mainly from the wild days when we had taken our bikes round on Mad Sunday, but I was not really familiar with the rest of it. And that meant that there were plenty of blind spots for me.

Rod, however, a real IOM race enthusiast, knew the entire course really well. He was always trying to teach me, but for some reason I just wanted to ride round it, never wanted to drive round in a car to have a steady look, or learn it as I really should have and as just about every other rider on the grid did. I just took it by each practice session, learning as I went. Anyway, however slack I had been about learning the track, I won the Newcomers' race, and set the fastest ever Newcomer record at the Manx with a lap of 116.66 mph. And that, really, was the start of my passion for road racing, and the foundations of my attitude as a racer.

It was tough, of course, and nobody had expected me to triumph over such a testing and exhausting track so early in my journey towards becoming a full-time racer. Riding the 600cc Honda I was up against all the bigger, faster 750 Suzukis as well. I remember reading *Motor Cycle News* when we were sailing out on the ferry. It had predicted that Jonathan Ralph, Alex Donaldson and John Burrows would be the front runners, and forecast Donaldson would probably win the Newcomers' race with Ralph second and Burrows third. They almost got it right, but not quite, because I won it. Jonathan was second, Alex third and John fourth. I was twenty-three years old and on my way to an Isle of Man race future that I could never have imagined would turn out to be so successful and so completely satisfying. In fact, record-breaking.

Today, when I see the newcomers, they have four or

five familiarisation tours being driven around in cars and minibuses, being talked through the circuit and instructed every yard of the way round by experts and retired riders, as well as spells watching on PlayStation or taking in all the videos they can. When I see them, I think... God, if only I had done all that. So now is a good time to ask, how many near misses have I had, in the beginning and nowadays?

None. I have never raced the course in crazy style. I have never been in that desperate a frame of mind. Obviously, 2015 disappointed me a bit, with photos in the press of me up the pavement in the Superstock race, because that was purely down the bike running out of fuel. Not my fault at all. I don't like anyone thinking that I ride like a madman around the course. I race it as fast but as safely as I can, but I'm not one of those guys who say to themselves, I am going to go out and do whatever it takes and kill myself if I have to. I am not like that. That is completely stupid and irresponsible. If someone wants to do that, then good luck to them. They will need it. You don't overstep the mark at the TT if you've got any brains. Sheer bravery and edgy daring don't come into it. Cool, rational thinking, allied to control and a complete understanding of your and the bike's limits around a track like the Isle of Man, do.

Between one TT and the next I don't even go around the place. During the races, I will get there ahead of official practice and do one lap to check where there are any new surfaces or likely problems. And that's it, one lap in a car.

That's all.

The course measures 37¾ miles, and constantly changes, the roads used every day by cars, buses, lorries. It used to be that everyone knew that down the Sulby Straight if you went over to the right there was a little bump, a little manhole, or that at the bottom of Bray Hill you had to take a line between the manhole cover and pavement edge. It seemed to me to be absolutely essential to remember all the perils and likely hazards and react by instinct developed from mental preparation and a photographic memory. Otherwise, on a track as dangerous as the TT, if you forget, you will be lucky . . . very lucky . . . if you get away with it

I think that a combination of instinct and memory comes from my early years on road bikes, and obviously developed with every road I went on.

Having ridden motorbikes since the age of seventeen, my awareness of the dangers is absolute. If you are any good as a rider, you reach that stage where you accept that you need to be aware of everything that is happening. I happen to have grown up sitting on motorbikes at 200-plus mph, learning as I have gone along, and the awareness of danger and the essential need to be wary have stayed with me. They will do as long as I am in this sport and competing at the level I do, against the best and most committed riders in the business.

I am competitive in some things, especially racing. Too competitive sometimes, which can take the fun out of an activity. My nature and instincts drive me to believe that I have got to be a winner, that you can't do anything, can't respect what you are striving to achieve over all the other guys equally committed (well nearly all of them . . .), unless you are a winner by sheer nature. That attitude and commitment can take the fun out of things sometimes. You might be away with the lads on some stag do and go go-karting and still do your best to win. I'm never there just for fun, I want to win. Whatever we do, I cannot help myself. It is my nature. My instinct. I see nothing wrong with that – and I would not change it. Besides, I think most bike racers have to be like that. That's what gets you across the line first on a Sunday afternoon . . . .

I do everything I can to be fit because I always feel that if you fail to win a race because your body is not up to the job, to the physical exertion, you should not bother to be a racer. My worst nightmare would be to be leading a TT and not be strong enough or fit enough to keep going as hard as I can, and then fail to finish in great form and get beaten at the end. I couldn't accept that. A crucial part of training really hard in winter is my attitude and my determination and commitment, the mental strength I need and have. Because you are doing stuff you don't want to do. It's horrible, a real test of your drive, training that hard. I think putting yourself through it every single day in winter makes you stronger. When you feel tired during a TT race you have actually been going through that in training all winter. I believe that is one of the biggest parts of it. The other side is that once your legs are too tired to lift yourself across onto your pegs you can't ride the bike as you should do. Some people may not even notice it, some people don't want to accept it because they don't want the team to know, but if you can't stand up on your footrests for six really tough and testing TT laps you are not going to be as fast for the finish as you were on lap one. If your shoulders are aching, if your arms are tired and can't muscle the bike around to get the best from its balance, it may be all right being able to relax in your saddle for one lap, but you need to be able to work yourself and the bike hard for six laps. That's purely down to fitness. Nothing less.

The idea of physical fitness doesn't necessarily occur to everyone – spectators when they look at racers may think, 'Oh he's on a motorbike. That's easy, he's being carried everywhere.' But, again, at the Isle of Man in particular, fitness and strength are the watchwords.

I don't accelerate my fitness levels in a specific build-up to the TT. I do all my training in winter and, if anything, back off a little beforehand because in the face of the island's tremendous challenge, you will be riding a bike every day. The TT is so physically demanding on you for two heavy weeks that the last thing you need to be doing is anything that might affect that.

As for diet, I'm not obsessed with it but I don't eat crap. I am not someone who delves into 'Let me find out exactly what I am supposed to eat at what time of the day.' I wouldn't do that. But I do also try to do my best to know what I should and shouldn't eat. That's common sense. Even so, my preparation, readiness and fitness are not obsessions to the point where I follow a harsh regime of a diet similar to, say, a lightweight boxer's, and I still eat what I enjoy but keep it sensible.

My training programme commits me to two hours a day in the gym for at least half of the winter. Then I am in there twice a day to undergo cardio in the morning and weights and strength work separately in the afternoon. It was my friend Martin Crosswaite, the trials rider, who got me into circuit training classes when I was around seventeen years old, so it has always seemed normal for me to be doing some training. I did circuit training for a lot of the early years of my racing, and then I had a personal trainer for 2007 when I rode for Honda. Since then I have worked with various different ones to try to work out what's best for me personally. I opt now for what I believe is the best and most beneficial from all the sessions I have undergone.

I think the difference nowadays – and it is hard to speak for other eras without sounding like you are putting someone down – can be seen in someone like Joey Dunlop, that truly great road racer who used to win TT races by a margin of a few minutes. Now we are winning races by a few seconds, so you cannot sit back on your talent in the hope that you will blitz everyone else on the last lap. How much fitness would have come into it if someone had been pushing the likes of

Joey every single second of every lap is a vital question, but any rider would need to do more fitness training to equip himself to beat a guy like that. When you have a lead of one or even two minutes on the last lap, your own fitness is less of a problem.

If we are not fully fit as racers, we can lap close enough to what we need to do, but someone else can get a lap in exactly the same as you, so somewhere along the line you are going to have to find something extra. The bikes are all so close in performance nowadays, unlike in the 1980s and 1990s, when there were considerable differences, so that there would often be a runaway winner because of the performance differentials.

For racers, there is also an overlap because fitness and concentration are closely linked. If you are not fit you can't concentrate; put simply, your concentration lapses if you have an ache somewhere. And if your concentration goes during a race you are likely to be off and up the road on your backside, especially in the island. In distance road racing, there is no question about that. Around the Isle of Man, to maintain that level of concentration at racing speeds for two hours or so is all important. Riders like John McGuinness are extra special in that they combine fitness and cool concentration with dash and daring, only taking chances when they are confident they can get away with them.

I have been really good friends with John for quite a while, from the days when I was doing team racing with

Honda in 2007. When not racing we would often go enduro riding together, spending a lot of time just enjoying each other's company. We were close friends for about four years, but since going through my scary leg injury and stuff, I don't have all that much to do with him any more. His achievements in the TT are massive and historic. That is an inescapable fact. But, to be honest, when I am asked if there is another rider I most appreciate I have to admit that there isn't. In all the time I have been racing there is no other rider I have actually admired and looked up to. I have done my own thing throughout my career because I have been keener to beat my rivals than look up to them. A case in point is Michael Rutter. We have had some fantastic clashes, some really close-fought battles, but off the track I have never had much to do with him. We have never really been friends, and by the same token I doubt that he would have much to say about me and my career.

Dean Harrison is still up and coming, and should improve with experience.

Then there is Guy Martin . . . I went through a long and hectic duel with him, especially in the races around Scarborough and the Ulster Grand Prix in 2006. Racing him at the Ulster was crazy. We both probably did stuff that pissed each other off a hell of a lot, and I guess I was probably as much to blame as he was. One time at the Ulster GP he tried to pass me on a little stretch of track where in my judgement there was no room. He had some scary moments, particularly at Scarborough, the place he thought he owned, skidding up the road, and close to killing himself. Mercifully we have both moved on a heck of a lot and Guy is actually a good rider. Very good, even if he does not have that last measure of ability to win races regularly.

As a racer, I think he is all right, but I don't think he is brilliant. Not by a long way. And I am certain that he is not as good as he imagines himself to be. McGuinness, though, is a terrific challenge. Hard, but as fair as can be. And you don't have to fret about flying elbows, boots or legs if you are side by side with him.

STEVE PARRISH

They are a double-act behind the TT scenes – but also a brilliant and informative pair upfront to millions of television viewers across the world. Their names? Steve Parrish – 'Stavros' to his friends – and James Whitham, both former racers around the Mountain course and ex-grand prix competitors.

They swapped their saddles for seats in the TV commentary box and being trackside for on-the-spot interviews, as pundits on the small box. And there is nobody better at the job of bringing the TT into the public eye, with a high level of expertise and honesty, than these two former British motorcycle race champions.

Steve, now sixty-three, ran in nine TTs (1975–7, 1981–6) without a win, and was more of an also-ran than a likely first-place rider in fifty-three grand prix starts. His vastly overshadowing Suzuki teammate, and best friend, was the legendary Barry Sheene, world champion in the 1977 500cc title chase. But what Steve failed to achieve on two wheels he more than compensated for when he switched to truck racing, in which he became the most successful driver of the heavy stuff in the world and its champion. As if that was not enough to keep him occupied he became a licensed pilot – and then opted to take up commentating on bike racing, firstly with BBC Radio before moving to Sky TV and then Channel 4.

One of his boasts is that he is credited in *The Guinness Book of Records* with achieving 'The Fastest Speed in Reverse' – going backwards at 85 mph in a Caterham sports car! He is a notorious practical joker famed for having his car number-plated PEN15. And when notorious party-goer and glamour boy Sheene was once so badly hungover that he could not ride, Steve disguised himself as the Suzuki number one in Barry's helmet and leathers, and qualified him to race. Then he put on his own gear – but finished further down the grid.

In his madcap days he earned a ban from Macau's Chinese Admin Region for blowing up a brothel with a home-made bomb assembled from fire crackers when he discovered some mates were inside sampling the benefits.

His last race was in 1985. He had logged fifty-two GPs with just one podium finish. A third place in the Senior

TT was scrubbed because he had an oversize tank. When Heron Suzuki sacked him in 1977 his great friend, Beatle George Harrison, said: 'Don't worry – I'll make sure you have enough tyres and petrol to keep racing on your own.' And he gave Stavros £55,000!

He, to me, is a natural broadcaster with plenty of confidence, but also the expertise and insight that are so crucial. As he says: 'Covering the TT is the most complicated form of television I have ever worked in. People do not realise how much work behind the scenes and in the planning goes into it.

'There are thirteen cameras around the course and another couple on the start line. The operators will film the leading riders through on lap one and then move on to another location to vary their shots as much as possible. When the race is over the course car will go round and stop at each location to pick up the disks from each camera and take them back to the our mobile studio at the Grandstand. Someone then ingests those disks into an editing suite and the edit begins. There are usually four or six editors and each one will do a lap each. Bear in mind that the disks won't make it back to the Grandstand until 4 p.m. and the show goes out at 9 p.m. Once the footage has been edited into chronological coverage of the race, we can go in and record our commentary. It's hard for us as commentators because we have no idea what we are going to see until we sit down to do it. And we are often still voicing at the end of the show while the programme has already started going out on TV. I always have to be up at the Grandstand by 8.30 a.m. and I don't get home until the show has finished transmitting, sometimes even later, so it stretches easily to twelve or thirteen hours' effort every day. But I honestly enjoy it. We make a one-hour programme every day of the TT. In between James and I do lots of little features and interviews, not only with the TT stars but also with people at the other end of the paddock who take two weeks off work and sleep in a tent just to go racing. Or we'll talk to the people who own the B&Bs, hotels, restaurants... in fact every aspect of life connected with the event. That is probably what wins us such big viewing figures. By the start of our second week of coverage we are getting close on a million viewers per show – and that's a greater audience than any other motorcycle race televised in the UK. So all our hard work is well worth the effort we so eagerly put into it. Jamie and I have a terrific working relationship and, all being well, it will continue for a good while to come. There cannot be too many jobs that are such a genuine treat to do and when you are as fired up about the TT, and those brave and spectacular competitors who leave us on the edge of our seats, as both of us are, then satisfaction is a completely natural result.

'I am now living my dream and having a ball. It is so nice to be involved like I am nowadays and I really do enjoy using my insight into this great sport as whatever you want to call me, a pundit or colour commentator.'

Steve's fifty-year-old partner in punditry is the very likeable Yorkshireman James 'Jamie' Whitham, with whom I've worked on his road-race tuition track days. In his racing heyday he was a regular winner and a British champion, voted 'Man of the Year' by *Motor Cycle News* readers in 1991 and again in 1996. And he deserved every single vote. He had to quit racing in 2002 suffering from glaucoma, the consequence, it seems, of his having undergone chemotherapy from when he contracted Hodgkin's Disease in 1995. Among other achievements and titles, he had by then amassed four World Supersport victories with twelve podiums, and in 1994 had raced alongside world champion Carl Fogarty, a good friend, in the World Superbikes series. Today, Jamie reckons that his best biking experience was winning the 750cc British championship double for Yamaha, and then hitting 185 mph around the awesome banking of the Daytona Speedbowl in Florida. 'Exhilarating,' was how he succinctly described that fabulous sensation.

'The problem with commentating on the TT is that you can't un-know something once you know it, and by the time we commentate on the races we already know what has happened. There was some debate about whether we should try to commentate as if it were live or just admit that we know what is going to happen. Eventually, we all decided it was more exciting and better to commentate on the races as if we are seeing them for the first time.' Of his commentating at the TT, he says:

'Working with Steve in the commentary booth is absolutely brilliant. Although he is a notorious prankster he is very professional and takes the job seriously so there is no problem there at all. But you have to be on the look-out for him and his antics when you are not working. You have to watch out for the pepper down the air vents in your car or you'll turn on the ignition and get a face full of the stuff. Or keep an eye open for the bucket of water balancing on top of your hotel door. And the jam in your trainers in the morning.

'One of the criticisms we get of our coverage is that we don't show enough of the riders further down the grid. But I always try to give backmarkers a name check if they are on the screen. Problem is, you are never going to be able to please all of the people all of the time – but I believe we do a fantastic job in capturing the flavour of the whole festival.'

CHAPTER 4

THE BINGLEY BULLET ON TARGET

O nce I started doing the Manx Grand Prix – the September challenge around the whole TT course, often in the most inclement weather – I began to get the really serious rides and team offers. So that's probably one of the most important stages of my racing career. From 2006 to 2010, and then my leg problems, make up the rest of the story. But let's go back a bit. In 2004 we were running the Suzuki that David Jefferies won as a bonus in 2002. He won three races for Suzuki, and he gave me one of the bikes to race the year after – so I had that for 2003 and 2004, and did the Superstock Championship and then obviously because I was going to the TT I heard about the North West 200. I had never known anything about the NW or the Ulster Grand Prix until, wanting to go to the TT, I picked up on them. So

I ended up road racing purely because I wanted to do the TT and those were the races you just did if you did the TT.

So I was riding for a team that was kind of based around the team that DJ rode for called Tech 2. DJ ran on purple and orange bikes in British Superstock but I think most of the team had fallen apart. I got a team together with another young rider. His dad was paying his bills and I built a 600 for him which I would use off the roads. And I had my 1000. We had a truck between us that the team had fixed us up with and it all came together with input from all over the place.

It was 2004. I went out to the NW 200 thinking I had all this team behind me and when I got there they set up all the awning and stuff and then left, to return for race day. So I had to go through all the practice on my own; I went out on the 600 for practice and by the time I had got a quarter into a 2-mile straight I was in the rev limit and in top gear. It was a Newcomers' practice and another young racer went off a cliff at Black Hill, falling right down the side of the cliff, so the race was delayed for some time while a sea rescue was organised for the hapless individual. I got back to the paddock, rushing to try and change the gearing on my 600. Before I knew it they were calling Newcomers up again. I was so scared of missing practice time as a Newcomer – you could go on any bike for the Newcomers' Race, but my Suzuki 1000cc would not be ready until later in the day. Even so, I ended up jumping on it with no tyre warmers, for the practice. I crashed at the first corner after only a few yards with cold tyres and put the bike into a wall, ending up in hospital. So that was my first year at the NW. A total disaster. I was in hospital with a fractured pelvis and my bike was absolutely wrecked.

I had come to know John McGuinness slightly by then and I remember leaving hospital a few days after the crash and going to collect my bike and he helped me lift the wreckage into the back of my truck.

My first ever TT was only about two weeks off, so it was quite a task to prepare for it. I got my bike out of its mess, and went to the island.

I did every class, 1000, Superbike, Honours Stock, Superstock and 600 on this Suzuki that I had built; I was eighth fastest in the final Junior TT practice session. But I managed only one top-ten finish – in the Formula One TT, edging out Manx rider Gary Carswell by 2.3 seconds after 150 miles of really hard work. I was sixteenth in the Senior but my air scoop fell off. I pulled over to fix it but I had to stop in the race.

Then in 2005 there was guy called Mark Johns who was going to run me on the roads, in Superstock and in the British Superbike Championship on a Honda, though the Honda Superstock bike wasn't the greatest bike at the time – the Suzuki S1000 was miles ahead. But it was my first time for a team and he was picking up the bills, pretty much all of them from what I can remember, and providing me with the bikes. All I had to do was just turn up to race. I was so looking forward to that year. But it was a total disaster. I crashed the Superstock bike a couple of times in the British Championships and I wrecked it at Thruxton and ended up not racing at all that weekend. I went to the NW and I can't even remember that race. I went to the TT and we had an oil leak in the Superbike pretty much for the whole of the fortnight. But I put together a CBR600 for Craig Atkinson who was in the Manx in September. The deal was I would build this good-spec 600 for him to race at the Manx if I could use it for the TT. He agreed. I managed three top tens and an eleventh place after getting into the top five in Superstock practice. But it was an up and down TT in all five events. After the TT I split with the team and went back to running my own Suzuki 1000 and doing British Superstock. I won a race towards the end of the year at Donington and I think it stood out to a lot of people because everyone knew I was there on my own – no team. I would just pull my bike out of the truck and go out and race it. Then. right out of the blue came a phone call from an Irish race team called McAdoo Racing, offering me bikes for 2006.

They had been doing really well with Ryan Farquhar, but he had moved on to TAS Suzuki. And I got offered his seat on their Kawasaki. I went out to see them. My tie-up with the McAdoo team was just for the roads, the NW, TT and Ulster. Brilliantly, our partnership was an immediate success, with two-way appreciation. For me it was the brand of big team I had always dreamed about and. They were going to pay for everything, for the bike and for the tyres. I wouldn't have to pay for anything to go racing. I don't know how it came about, I feel cheeky now looking back at it, but I used to have my own workshop then and I had gone through a bad year with Mark Johns with our bikes being a disaster. I suggested to McAdoo that I would ride for them if they supplied me road bikes and paid for all the bits so I could build them myself. I am surprised they didn't tell me to piss off there and then. They went along with it and they actually paid me as my workshop to build the bikes for them as well.

That was my breakthrough for getting a ride for a team They were great to work with and ride for. I repaid them with some committed effort. I went and did the Cookstown 100. I didn't really want to do any other road races, but the team owner, Winston McAdoo, lives on the circuit. It clashed with Oulton Park and I remember flying back and forth in between. I actually set pole position on the Superstock bike for the Superbike race – never having seen Cookstown before – and won the 600 race. I would have won the Cookstown 100 race but on my last lap Martin Finnegan ran into the back of me and he fell and ran me straight up the slip road. I think I finished third or fourth. I really enjoyed my time there.

I then went straight on to the North West 200. A disaster. I slid off on the first 600 – one we had built with a standard road bike gearbox and the first gear was way too tall and we had to slip the clutch to get moving in first gear. The first 600 race, coming out of the roundabout I slid off – I was absolutely devastated. No injury – the bike skidded up the road. I walked all the way back thinking how I'd got this big chance and had blown it. I was devastated. Utterly. I told myself at least I was lucky not to be hurt, but that was small consolation. I walked all the way back to the paddock feeling miserable every yard of the way and blaming myself for blowing this golden opportunity to break into the big time with a great team. But I managed to get my act together for the Superstock and broke the lap record and finished second to the New Zealander Bruce Anstey. Then I climbed back aboard the 600 for a win. So it all turned out well, to the great joy of the McAdoos.

The TT was next up. I ended up on the podium for every race in which I competed, apart from the Senior in which I broke down, with two second places and a third – although one of the runners-up spots was denied me because my Kawasaki ZX-6 was deemed illegal due to a 0.2mm difference in the cam dimensions.

I managed a repeat show at the Ulster Grand Prix, losing out to Guy Martin in both Supersport races.

Racing for Winston McAdoo and his son Jason was an absolute joy. We all got on so well together. They were a very religious family, going to church every Sunday, which meant they would never race their bikes on the Sabbath. I suppose because I didn't really appreciate the strength of their beliefs, and viewed them as odd, and because I was a mad keen biker, I did not fully understand their attitude and I may have suspected they were not as keen as they could have been on motorcycle racing. How wrong could I be? They absolutely loved their racing and put in endless hours of effort. Winston was a terrific and likeable bloke – he is still at every race now and always comes and says hi.

My career was heading just the way I wanted it to go. Winston McAdoo was saying he would be able to give me some money to ride for him the year after. And what's more, big names and team bosses were starting to sit up and take notice. The Bingley Bullet, as I became dubbed, was right on target. I was still living at home with my parents. I was twenty-six and didn't have a penny in the bank. I also had £30,000 debt on credit cards, all built up through my racing costs and having to pay for tyres and everything that went wrong with my bikes. If I crashed I would be in dead trouble. I would never have been able to clear my debts. Then, like a dream come true, I was in the money. I returned from the TT and wrote out a cheque to clear every single credit card. Wow! That was the real start of it all for me. And there was more to come. Much more.

I was doing my stuff in the British Championship, and one morning while I was at the Croft Circuit I received a phone call. I had not yet got up and was barely awake. I had to clear my throat and answer nicely and pretend I was not still in my kip. It was a voice I had never heard before, a guy I had never met, one of the biggest names in motorcycle racing, I couldn't believe when he said who he was: Neil Tuxworth. Clearly, my name was being bandied about behind the scenes at the big-time teams. He wanted me to call in on him at the team truck for a chat. Neil Tuxworth of all people. Mega!

Neil's reputation as the Honda race boss in the UK was tremendous. He had been a rider himself until a crash wrecked his career. From being a kid cycling to Cadwell Park to watch the races and, as a fourteen-year-old, helping out clearing up litter and looking after the flags for the marshals, he was hooked. His own TT career had him taking on the Isle of Man's challenge sixty-six times with a best finish of a second. He took up team management when the injuries he sustained in a serious accident cut short his motorcycle-racing days. His TT fascination gripped him and up to today, mainly with his backing and know-how, Honda is the top-scoring manufacturer of all time on the island with more than 250 victories. He has overseen wins by all-time legends Joey Dunlop, Carl Fogarty, Steve Hislop and John McGuinness. He says he has revelled in so many fantastic memories, with so many successes adding to Honda's incredible record, that it is impossible to pick out a special one.

It was seeing my TT shows, pepped up by my Ulster Grand Prix showing, that triggered his interest in me. From my standpoint it was an essential breakthrough. I think he wanted me riding for them not so much for me to win for them but for me not to beat them on a bike that wasn't a Honda. I would never have told him, but I would have ridden for Honda and him for free. All I ever wanted to do, just like every other motorcycle racer, was race on a Honda. I used to walk up and down the paddock just looking at their bikes and their set-up, dreaming that one day I might get a ride with somebody like them.

I really loved riding for Winston McAdoo and he told me he would be able to pay me some money for the following season. But I could not resist meeting up with Neil and listening to what he had on his mind and what plans he might have for me. I won't go into the figures, but he outlined an offer for me to ride for him the next year that excited me beyond belief. Somehow, don't ask me how, I managed to control myself and keep a straight business face and stance. But despite my excitement at his offer of the ride, and his promise of what the team would offer in support, I was a bit disappointed by how much he was offering to pay me. He said he would have a re-think and get back in touch. He phoned me the next day with an improved offer – and, again, maybe stupidly, and certainly cheekily, I said it was not yet what I had in my mind as to my worth. I mentioned my own figure and he said there was no way he could match it because his budget could not cope. I left the problem with him and decided it was a risk I should take without backing off. A good few anxious days passed. Neil said he would talk it over at the upcoming race at Cadwell. But he never did. Silverstone was the next chance we had for a further discussion. Nothing. But some time after that, at another race, he called me into his office, right at the end of the day, and, to my delight and relief, offered me rides in the British Supersport championship, the North West 200, the Ulster and the TT in all classes, plus a fee that left me happy, a car and a motocross bike. Needless to say, I took up his offer. And it was all my own decision. I did not have an agent or manager or anybody to guide me through the maze of contracts and dealings. In this instance I didn't need one: I knew this was my dream come true. A Honda ride. A sensational winning team. Full backing behind the scenes. And with superb guiding light Neil Tuxworth as my boss. I could not have wished for more. I was now on the brink of the big time and I felt ready, willing and very able to answer all the challenges and pressures I was bound to be facing as an HM Plant Honda factory rider.

That was the start of the real dream becoming reality. Also I had to start working hard because I was getting paid to ride motorbikes. And suddenly I was in the big time.

I was *expected* to get results. It was not a case of just *wanting* to get them. So the whole scene changed. I did everything I could to fulfil everybody's and my own ambitions – I even got a personal trainer that winter and put in as much effort as I possibly could.

I was twenty-seven. I bought a motorhome to live in over the racing at the weekends and probably started to get a little more extravagant!

Suddenly, I was now a full-time, full-blooded professional with a fierce determination to be the best in the business and, now, with some of the finest equipment and backing to achieve my dreams.

My financial life picked up. I still had some prize money left from 2006, and when I started to get my salary from Honda I bought a Hummer H2 car – a humungous thing but I think it was one of those things I just had to buy . . . I had never had anything that good in my life. I just thought I have always wanted one – now I can afford it. So go for it!. It became a bit of a joke – 325 hp, 6.0 litre, 3000 kg and 12 mpg: it cost about £1 per mile to run. But that was the first and pretty much the only extravagant thing I did.

So by now, with my pay packet and the rest of the stuff I was in pretty good shape financially.

And I was getting a fee, appearance money, to go to the North West, the TT and Ulster from the organisers.

I never had a manager because I preferred to do my own bargaining and arguing. I never knew where to be with the business side of the sport at first and it has taken a lot of years to figure it out. But I still don't truly think that the real front runners nowadays are getting what money they should do. It's a difficult subject.

That's life, you have to work out what you are worth. You say I don't exaggerate my worth but this is what I think I am worth so you must pay me that and I agree with that 100 per cent and you should still do it. That's the way it works.

Signing for HM Plant Honda for British Supersport was my big aim. I had started off doing Superstock and doing all the circuits and not as a road racer, and I really wanted to be a short-circuit racer and I wanted to try to win the Supersport Championship. I got what was the equivalent of a factory Supersport ride this year and it started off really tough; it was a brand-new model and with new forks, still being developed. I struggled with the bike and I struggledfor really good results. I was in the top ten but not as high as I felt I should be, and I was finding it hard. At Oulton Park I got knocked off going down Cascades and damaged my left shoulder. I couldn't lift my arm up so I couldn't race on the Monday at Oulton – and I was due to race at the North West 200 a day later. Neil Tuxworth warned me that if I needed any painkilling injections I was not racing at the NW. As far as I was concerned there was no question of my not going to the NW – I just *had* to be there: it was my run on the Superbike and everything for the TT build-up. So I fibbed and said I would be all right, my shoulder was just bruised. I went to the NW and somehow got my way through – but the qualifying was a calamity because the flywheel on the Superbike sheared off and came out of the crankcase and poured oil everywhere. As a result I missed the whole qualifying session so I had to start on the back row of the grid. I remember sitting around with some Irish privateer bikes and my factory HM Plant Honda motorcycle was a work of art compared with the other motorcycles surrounding me. What a catastrophe this is turning out to be, I thought. On race day I went and got a painkilling injection from the doctor without telling Neil – I had to, I was in so much pain. Even so, the NW was a disaster because of my shoulder and I didn't really get any results.

We came away from the NW and I had about a week before the 2007 TT. I had my motorhome, McGuinness had a motorhome, Michael Rutter had a motorhome and all three of us decided to go straight to the TT from the NW, so as to have a week of fun on the Isle of Man before the race started. We had the greatest week ever as build-up to the TT. We went out drinking every night, partying and generally having a lot of fun. It was something I would never do now. Mad. We should never have done it. But it helped the three of us relax. And easing the pressure, I think, helped me relax for a superb week's racing. John McGuinness and I were the only two riders to finish on the podium for every single race. In a practice run, I was recorded at 192.838mph through the Sulby Speed Trap – a speed I was not to match in the actual races. I was on the podium four times, finishing third in both Superbike events, third in the Superstock, and achieved my first victory there during a really hard-fought four-lap Supersport Junior TT, when I beat John McGuinness by a mere 2.84 seconds. And what a race! Bruce Anstey, brilliant at the IOM, was the leader on his Suzuki until a pit stop problem with his engine lost him 23 seconds. McGuinness, another TT master, took over on lap three but by Glen Helen I had replaced him up front by one-third of a second and then I pulled out an advantage of 5.03 seconds by the end of the lap. McGuinness, with typical fighting spirit and determination, cut my lead to 2.8 seconds by the Bungalow on the last lap. And it was a real test of my own attitude and skill to hang on to my lead for my debut triumph. But I did and clinched it, with my teammate but big rival John coming second. A Honda 1-2-3 was completed by Guy Martin. Anstey made it into fourth place. The 2007 TT season had lived up to my hopes.

I was the only HM Plant bike out there, so I felt quite a bit of pressure with that situation. To win it felt amazing. I came back from there loving life. And the 600 in the British title chase started to pick up a bit. Later in that season I also won the Ulster Grand Prix in the Superbike class – but could only end up eighth in the British Supersport title chase, including beating John McGuinness to first place, on a wet track, at Oulton Park for Bike Animal Honda.

I won a wet race at Oulton Park, and the season was outstandingly starting to take favourable shape. Even so, there were problems. I led the race at Cadwell Park, before crashing out and totalling the bike. It was a bad weekend for the team, as my teammate Leon Camier also crashed on the infamous Mountain section and spectacularly broke his leg; it looked horrific. After the weekend Neil Tuxworth called me in and said he'd like me to ride the Superbike for the last two rounds, which was an amazing opportunity for me. But I really liked the 600 and was looking forward to another year on it. I wanted to finish the season on it and said I would do it if I could ride my 600 as well, but they wouldn't have that. They just wanted me to ride the Superbike. I was up the road at the end of the year, which was devastating for me, as I had thought everything was going to be brilliant for the year to come with Honda. I had thought I had a genuine chance at the 600 title for the year to come. I think that was kind of the end of me ever really being able to make a short-circuit racer because I was twenty-seven by then. And I felt I could have won the Supersport Championship the next year, which would have led me on to doing Superbikes. I was just up and down and all over the place.

I ended up riding in 2008 for Alistair Flanagan's AIM Racing Yamaha team – and it was probably my worst year of racing motorcycles *ever*. I did get some results but the bike was just breaking down everywhere. And it always seemed to be my bike, nothing ever happened to my teammate's bike. In the British Championship I was struggling all the time, with teammate Steve Plater running at the front. We went to the North West 200 and my Superbike was horrendous. In qualifying, the back wheel collapsed, the bearing broke and the disc shattered and hit me on the back of the head at 180 mph. Luckily, I got away with it. In the 600 race Steve and I were miles ahead. We must have been 10 or 15 seconds up the road with one of us up for the win. Just as I was going to lead the race my engine blew up. It just went on and on like this. So frustrating. At the TT I broke down one night on the 600 and then the Superbike burst into flames in the paddock. I just could not believe the non-stop setbacks and utter catastrophes. The upshot was that I should quit. I walked away telling them, This is it – I'm out of here. I told them I was going home. I remember John McGuinness concernedly chasing me round to the awnings. He had no reason to be trying to help me out but he came running after me telling me to keep my chin up and that I would be all right. But I was distraught and I said: 'This is all just a joke, John – I can't be riding bikes at a TT with all this going on.' He responded: 'You ride your 600 every week, go and do a couple of laps on that and enjoy it. Sit down and get your Superbike sorted tonight.' His supportive attitude was positive and he talked me into going back – I would have gone home that night.

I set off on my 600 and tried to get my mind right. I got as far as Greeba Castle and nearly had the biggest highside ever at the TT. I have never had a moment there but it was either a puncture or the back tyre had suddenly gone flat. I just thought, Bloody hell, this is a never-ending disaster. I am going to end up dead at this TT. Anyway, against all my instincts, I put up with it and carried on for the first Superbike race. I remember coming up to the paddock and seeing this really strange device on my oil filler on the Superbike and I was asking what is this, and they said the bike's using too much oil so we need to put some in: 'Don't worry about it, ignore it.' I said, 'If we have to put some oil in it then we shouldn't be messing with oil things at a TT, it doesn't sound right . . .' and they said not to worry, that it was used all the time, and that I should just get on with what I needed to do. I did the first laps and I was running in the top three or four and came in for a pit stop. They topped up the oil and filled the bike with fuel. I set off down Bray Hill and my foot slipped off the peg. I looked down and this thing that was meant to top up the oil was gone. It had broken. So all the oil had come out.

I ended up breaking down in that race, because of this oil problem. I was really fed up, and then in the first 600 race I broke down again, while I was ahead of Steve Plater, who went on to win the race. A lot of riders broke down. Steve had been going up the pecking order as people quit with mechanical issues, and finished second. Then the winner, Bruce Anstey, was disqualified so Steve ended up winning the race for AIM Yamaha. Which just made it even worse from my side. It looked as though it was me not the bikes. In the second race Steve broke down and I was on the podium with second place. I think that was the first breakdown Steve had had at the team. In the Senior race I managed to secure a third place. But yes, that TT was what I class even now, all this time distant, as a total disaster that never let up and got worse and worse.

The weekend right before the Ulster Grand Prix I was at

Knockhill, and because Steve was doing a World Endurance race they brought a Scottish rider in for the weekend, and this kid had done well whereas I had been struggling in wet practice and qualifying.

We had gone out for morning warm-up and my bike was horrendous. The back kept coming round on me everywhere. I couldn't tip into the first corner so I came in to ask what was wrong. I got them to check the tyre pressure and there was 50 psi in the rear tyre. So they lowered it to the right pressure and I finished the morning warm-up. Then I came back in and said I can't do this any more. I packed it in and left the team. That was the end of it. I wasn't going to the Ulster Grand Prix. However, the race organisers were disappointed that I was going to be absent and asked if I would still come out and just do some publicity stuff for them. So I caught the ferry to go out there. In the meantime they had been trying to get me a bike and had spoken to Rob McElnea, who was running Yamahas, and had done a deal with him so that I could ride Carl Harris's Superbike and a 600 from their team.

All this came about without me ever even speaking to Rob. I think Alistair Flanagan at AIM thought all this had been set up beforehand, when I had walked out on him at Knockhill. But that was absolutely not the case. I was going to the Ulster just to do some PR stuff. The organisers were working really hard on getting me bikes because they wanted me out there, and it was they who made a deal with Rob to get me to race. The first time I spoke to him was when he rang me to talk me through what I would be riding. As I got to the Ulster, a massive Yamaha truck turned up with two beautiful bikes, and I thought I am back and going again. But the weather was horrendous and the whole event got cancelled, so I never got to race. As winter approached Rob sat me down and we looked at what we could do for the year after, and he agreed to run me on a Superbike with Chris Walker. It would be me and Chris on British Superbikes so I was excited again. But then Rob called me in again and said maybe it's better if we just run you on the 600. I was getting the vibe that he had no interest in the roads and he wasn't going to give me the opportunity that I wanted for British Superbikes. I said I think we should probably just leave it.

It was now January of 2009, I had no ride at all. That's when the Padgett's situation all set off, really. I jumped on my pushbike and cycled over to see Clive Padgett because Honda decided they were coming back to the TT for 2009 and I knew they had a Superstock, a Superbike and a 600 that were current models, and that John McGuinness was going back to Honda. I told Clive I would be interested in running on the roads, and he said he would like to have me in the team but I wouldn't be getting any money for it, and I wouldn't be riding anything in the British Championships because he already had his two 600 riders lined up. But I was really keen for the chance to ride his machines and agreed to his offer.

We went on and did an OK job at the North West 200

– not the best with two sixth places. But at the TT I fared much better with two wins out of three solo races – the Superstock and Supersport events. I thought I would have a good chance of winning the second 600 race as well, but it rained on the Wednesday and I wasn't up much for a wet race at the TT so we didn't win the second one. I was in fifth place for that. In the Senior, just when I looking a dead cert for a podium finish I ran over some oil at Quarter Bridge and slid off. That spillage lost me the chance to pocket £10,000 prize money as the most successful rider of the week. It was won by Steve Plater and I ended second in the championship standings on 74 points, 10 adrift of Steve.

Obviously Clive and I got a good relationship going together, and I went on for the rest of the year and ended up doing some Superstock races. I won a Superstock race at Oulton for him and also did some Supersport races, and there was no doubt that I was going to stay racing with Clive. I had a really good time racing with him and I was back having fun again and getting results. We discussed a lot about the Superbike particularly because I had struggled with that bike, and we went into that winter doing a lot of work to get the bike right for the following year.

I started 2010 doing the 600 Championship for him with Glen Richard, who was the current British Supersport champion from riding a Triumph the year before. I think that year was my kind of proof that I could have made it as a short-circuit racer as well, because my teammate was the current Supersport champion and now he was on exactly the same bike as me and he only beat me once all year, at Snetterton.

We struggled with bikes in the British Championship – Clive was just running a kit bike on quite a small budget and we were up against teams with full-blown electronics and really good bikes. We were struggling to win and getting frustrated – I had crashed out of second place at Mallory, and suggested not riding a 600 any more that year because I just wanted to do the Superstocks; I didn't think the other bikes were competitive enough. Clive promised to get better electrics for it, and it went on like that. But for the road racing it went really well and we had a good North West, and, leading into the TT, I knew I had every chance of winning any of the races there. I finished up fastest in practice week on the Superbike and I think people know most of the details of what happened throughout that TT. But that doesn't stop me reminding them!

CLIVE PADGETT

If there is a name automatically associated with achievement and success at the TT it is undoubtedly that of Padgett. And Clive Padgett in particular, an inspiration if ever there was one, especially to riders who find themselves under his guidance and towering expertise for the extreme challenge that is the world's toughest road race. The family bike business, based in Yorkshire, is the foundation of Clive's background as a race-team boss. And as a former racer himself, the youngest ever British champion, with lap records all over the place and a win aboard a 250cc Yamaha in only his first race in 1976, his deep understanding of all our needs as racers is unmatched. The Padgett heritage, the bike sales business itself, began with brothers Peter and Don in 1958, when they were tied in with Honda, Suzuki and

Yamaha, the Japanese manufacturers who reshaped the motorcycle market.

Clive's maxim was, and still is: to be successful you must set your sights on the top. Second place is never enough. Padgett's Racing became the most successful privateer team in the world, chasing and capturing glory on home-built machines and attracting world-class riders and champions like Mike Hailwood, his pal Bill Ivy, Phil Read, Rob McElnea, Ron Haslam, Carl Fogarty, Bruce Anstey, John McGuinness – and me. In the last thirty-nine TT races that the team has started, they have netted thirty-three top-four finishes, and of those twenty-seven were podium places and eleven were wins – a win rate of better than 25 per cent. They have won a TT race in every decade since the 1960s.

In the programme for the 2016 TT, Stu Barker penned a fine tribute to Clive under the headline 'Few Men Are More Passionate About the TT than Clive Padgett', with the sub-heading: 'Hutchy Alone Won SEVEN TT's in TWO Years on Our Bikes'. Here it is:

Perhaps the most impressive of all was the team's performance at the 2010 TT when they became the first outfit in TT history to win all five main solo races. The odds against Ian Hutchinson's Padgett's-prepared Honda CBR600RR and CBR1000RR Fireblade (in Superstock and Superbike trim) not suffering any mechanical mishaps in over 900 racing miles around the world's most demanding racetrack must have been astronomical, yet the Padgett's bikes never missed a beat. If there was an award for the single greatest achievement in TT history then this outrageous feat would surely be in contention.

'If you had asked me before 2010 if I thought that was ever possible I would have said no,' Clive readily admits. 'I don't think anyone thought it was possible. There had been over a hundred years of TT racing at that point and no one had ever achieved that. I still get speechless now when I think about it. It was just one of those incredible things. The following year Bruce Anstey was leading the Superbike race until a valve chipped and spoiled his race. But we won the Supersport event on the Monday so we very nearly did seven in a row! Hutchy alone won seven TTs in two years on our bikes, which isn't bad going!'

Strangely for a team with such a long and proud heritage at the TT, no one at Padgett's (or Valvoline Racing by Padgett's Motorcycles, as the team is officially known since it secured a title sponsor in 2014) actually knows how many races the team has won in total. 'I honestly don't know,' Padgett laughs. 'I always cover that question by saying we've won TTs in every decade since the 1960s, but I don't know the real total. We are a forward-looking team so our focus is always on the next race rather than looking back.'

Padgett's of Batley in West Yorkshire is one of the best-known motorcycle dealers in the country. Founded in 1958, an involvement with racing began almost immediately as Clive's father Peter took up the sport and found the perfect way to mix business with pleasure. Peter is still heavily involved in the family business and still works six days a week, but has been aided in the intervening years by his brother Don, Clive himself, and Clive's brother Alan and sister Cath. Clive's other brother, Gary, won the Formula 3 TT in 1982 and the Production Class C race four years later, but tragically he lost his life in a road accident just nine days after winning his second TT.

Clive raced, too, and was another red-hot talent on a racing motorcycle, but his career was cut short far too early by injury. In his very first season in 1977 he won the 250cc and 500cc ACU Clubmans championships, and the 250cc Gold Star British championship. With results like that he was fast-tracked to grands prix for 1978 and managed a top-six finish in his debut season before suffering career-ending injuries at the Belgian round at Spa-Francorchamps.

Since then, he has focused his competitive spirit on his race team and has worked with some of the greatest road racers of modern times, including John McGuinness, Bruce Anstey, Ian Hutchinson and Cameron Donald. Going further back in time other notables Padgett's have supplied bikes for are Hailwood, Ivy, Read, Fogarty, McElnea and Haslam. The team's list of former riders reads like a *Who's Who* of British motorcycle racing.

Even so, Clive says, 'It is quite incredible how competitive the racing is right now.' He knows, though, that it is an accepted fact that a happy rider is a fast rider. 'Everyone who works in our team are friends – they are not just people who have dropped a CV through the door,' Padgett adds, 'we all eat together, we all go for a pint together – and the whole thing has to gel. That is a huge part of our friendly family team.'

It is this tight-knit family atmosphere that defines the Padgett's team, both on the racing side and in the showroom. 'The race team operates separately from the showroom staff but we always get help from the staff in the shop – the storesman will help, so will the secretary, the delivery driver, too, will help. The race team is integral and has its own staff but there are so many others in the building who help out. Everybody at Padgett's is passionate about racing motorcycles. I mean, the girl in the front office has worked with us for thirty-three years, since she was a fifteen-year-old Saturday girl, and she still always texts me to find out about the racing. It is fabulous how passionate everybody is.'

Although Padgett's team has campaigned various makes of bikes over the years (Padgett's Yamaha was a particularly successful partnership in the 1980s) Honda has been the marque of choice for some time now – although the engines used by the team are tuned in-house. But given how many times they have beaten the official factory Honda effort at the TT in recent years, does not Honda get just a little miffed?

'We've got a great relationship with them,' says Clive, 'it was lovely to see our team winning one of the big races last year [2015], Anstey in the RST Superbike, and the official Honda team winning the other with McGuinness in the PokerStars Senior, but I can't really answer the question. You would have to ask Honda that.'

In 2010 Padgett's stole the entire show at the TT, taking those unprecedented five wins in one week with Ian Hutchinson – Superbike, Superstock, Supersport races one and two, and the Senior. But after such an astonishing week, doesn't that mean the team will always leave the TT feeling slightly disappointed if they don't win every race?

Not according to Clive. 'I don't think I have ever left the TT feeling disappointed and that is simply because I love it so much. Just to be at the event, to be stood on the Glencrutchery Road, is always a special feeling. You've got to go there and, first of all, hope that everyone has a safe fortnight. Anything after that is a bonus.

'Luckily, we have managed to be competitive, too. So, while some years are better than others in terms of results, we are never disappointed at the end of a TT. Results are not exactly secondary to us but first and foremost we go to the TT to have fun and enjoy ourselves.

'Ask anyone why they started riding motorcycles in the first place and you will always get the same answer... for pure enjoyment. It is the same with TT racers – they don't go for the first time to try and win it, they go to compete in it and enjoy it. Only after that do their aspirations build. But you have to enjoy it to get results. A happy rider there is a fast rider.'

The reliability that Padgett's worked into Ian Hutchinson's bikes in 2010 was extraordinary. None of them missed a beat all week, and that's something Clive puts down to experience. 'We've all been brought up around motorcycles and during a normal week away from the TT we work on everything from 50cc scooters to Honda Gold Wings. Our team is so experienced, and I am not being funny here, but if you look in our garage there is not a man under the age of forty. But I mean that as a compliment. It means they are all hugely experienced. Another huge plus point is that all our team, apart from one man, has actually raced bikes. That is a big thing in understanding the requirements of the bikes we prepare to race and wishes and needs of our riders.'

Hutchy's fab five in a week. Could it be done again? Could there ever be another clean sweep at the TT? Clive believes so and he says: 'Yes. If it has been done once then there is no reason it cannot happen again. People get holes-in-one twice in golf, don't they? But it is not easy and I don't know if my nerves could take it again! We are not one of those teams that says we are going to do this and that.'

He adds matter-of-factly, 'We will just arrive on the Isle of Man and go for it.'

Incidentally, for those keen-eyed among you who may have spotted that Padgett bikes always carry a sticker bearing the name 'Fiona' on the front mudguards Clive explains:

'Fiona is my youngest daughter. She's twenty-four now but she's had her sticker on our bikes since she was little. It was her idea. And you will see on the backs of some of the seats Lexi-Blake. That's my granddaughter, my eldest daughter Helen's girl. It just extends the family feel of our team. It's all done to put a smile on a little girl's face. And it has caught on. We have customers buying Padgett replica bikes wanting their kids' names on them too. We even had one guy asking to put the name 'Bruno' on his bike and when

I asked if it was his son he said 'No, it's my dog.' It looks like we have started a trend.'

CHAPTER 5

2010:
THE FAIRY-TALE TT

It was a bizarre and oddball TT, really: everything was going so well with every bike and I was in a good place and enjoying racing and Clive Padgett was great to work for. We were having fun – we were having fun and winning races. My first year on Clive Padgett's team started brilliantly. Ahead of the 2010 TT I had a decent run at the North West 200 where I came second, after Alistair Seeley and followed by Michael Dunlop, in the Supersport; first in the second Supersport, with Keith Amor and Bruce Anstey taking second and third place respectively, and another runner-up place in the Superstock behind Keith Amor and followed by Ryan Farquhar. To me it seemed a perfect rehearsal for the big Manx show to come.

Then it was on to the Isle of Man. Looking back, the practice week seems to have presaged that memorable winning streak: I clocked 130.6 mph during one practice session – though, to be honest, I was surprised not to have been beaten as conditions were perfect for fast laps. And my luck held out. On Saturday, 5 June I won my first Superbike race – my fourth TT win to date. Michael Dunlop, a formidable rival, came second, and Cameron Donald took third place. On Monday morning I won the Supersport race, with Guy Martin and Michael Dunlop taking second and third places. And in the afternoon I won the Superstock, ahead of Ryan Farquhar and Conor Cummins. That day I thought, It doesn't get any better than winning two TT races in one day. To win a TT was, and is, massive. To win two races in one day made it, so far, the best day of my life at the TT.

But as the day of my next race – Wednesday – dawned I was put in mind of the Wednesday race in 2009 when a wet race put paid to my chances of a win. This year too it rained. The weather was horrendous and it was wet all round the course. Even so, the organisers were talking about the feasibility of running the event, which I thought was crazy. I just said, 'Well, if you run today I'll be down at the bottom of Bray Hill watching. I won't be in it.' I did not mean that as a way of forcing them to stop the race – it was simply that I was not going to race in the wet. Luckily, they postponed the race until the day after when

Classic Isle of Man TT scenery: Hutchy in action on the Team Traction Control Yamaha
in the Supersport 2 race, 10 June 2015. He won at 125.803 mph. *(© Tim Keeton)*

Above: The most embarrassing photo ever: me and my dad on trials bikes, which is how it all started. As you can see, we didn't have a clue.

Below: Proud as punch on my first road bike: me on my Yamaha TZR250SP outside my parents' house. I crashed it on my first visit to the Isle of Man while trying to pull a wheelie . . .

Above: The lads I met while working at Appleyard's who became my best friends and riding companions, and with whom I first travelled to the island. Sitting on the banking at Rhencullen during the 1999 TT Races.

Below: 'I suggested that we should just get some cheap 600cc race bikes and go and do some cup racing.' From left to right: me, Matt Dobbins and Craig Atkinson at our first club race at Mallory Park.

Above: Before the accident: me on the Padgett's Racing Honda at the 33rd Milestone, with the record five trophies that I won at the TT that year.

(© Stephen Davison)

Right: Back in leathers, for the Arai parade lap to mark the centenary of the TT, June 2011. Beneath the covering on my left leg is the metal frame that held it all together.

(© Stephen Davison)

Above: Grit, determination and a relentless fitness programme were to pay huge dividends following my crash at Silverstone in September 2010.

Inset: My left leg, at some point during the long surgical and rehabilitation process needed to save it.

Below: 'I then took a crazy course of action' – material I used to mould round my leg to make a carbon fibre cast so that I could go racing again. It worked.

Above: Return to winning ways: on my way to victory in the 2013 Macau Grand Prix on Shaun Muir's Milwaukee Yamaha.

(© Stephen Davison)

Below left: At Brands Hatch in 2014, a forgettable racing year for me.

(© PA Images/Nigel French/EMPICS Spor

Below right: A rare moment of relaxation at home in Yorkshire.

(© Stephen Davison)

Left: With, from left to right, Guy Martin, Conor Cummins and Michael Dunlop at the premiere of the film *TT3D: Closer to the Edge* in London, April 2011.

(© Getty Images/Ferdaus Shamim)

Below: John McGuinness accepts the trophy for the 2009 Superbike TT from Valentino Rossi, the multiple MotoGP world champion. McGuinness now has twenty-three TT wins.

(© Pete Williamson/AP/PA Images)

Above: 'After a near five-year battle back to fitness, and as many as thirty different operations, an emotional Hutchy was initially unable to speak in the post-race press conference, but he eventually regained his composure to admit that his victory was very special.' My first of three wins during the 2015 TT.

(© Stephen Davison)

Below: My first TT win since my five victories in 2010 and my accident: me after the first Supersport race, 8 June 2015.

(© Tim Keeton)

bove: Guy Martin follows my line during the Senior TT, 12 June 2015. McGuinness on at 130.48 mph, with James Hillier second and me in third.

elow: In action during Northern Ireland's North West 200 race, May 2016.

Above: With my parents at the RAC's clubhouse in Pall Mall, London, in January 2016, after being awarded the Torrens Trophy for 'outstanding determination and courage in overcoming adversity to win multiple TT races'.

Below: A shot taken after it was announced that I would race for Tyco BMW in 2016. The S1000RR bikes are superb; in the Isle of Man that year they never missed a beat.

Above: Performing a burn-out after securing Tyco BMW's first win at the Ulster GP, August 2016 . . .

Below: . . . And on the podium, holding the sign announcing my outright record lap of 134.089 mph.

(© Stephen Davison)

Walking back to the paddock with another trophy, this time after the third race of the 2015 TT. During this, my comeback year to the TT, I had three more wins. *(© Stephen Davison)*

the weather was beautiful and we all had a great race and broke a lot of records. I won my fourth TT of the year – the second Supersport race – beating Michael Dunlop by 1.4 seconds (Keith Amor coming up behind him), and equalling Phillip McCallen's 1996 record of four wins in a week. It was at this point that I started to feel the pressure for Friday. I knew it was going to be the hardest race to win, and, especially against John McGuinness who put almost his whole TT effort into the Senior race. I was aching and tired and mentally strained from the feeling that I was now obliged to lead every night in practice week and to win every race – but I had to go and give it my best shot against the odds.

You always struggle a bit with sleep, especially in practice week because you are out from 6 p.m. to 8 p.m. and you do a debrief with your team and you don't get to eat until 9 or 9.30 p.m. and go to bed on a belly full of food. Then, in bed, all the laps on three different bikes are flying through your head as you try to work out what bike was doing what. It is hard to sleep under those stressful circumstances. Virtually impossible. But that was the way it was and I just had to get on with it. On top of all that it was back to back as well: we raced on Thursday and went straight into the Senior the day after with no rest, so I knew it was going to be hard day. I set off the line but within half a lap my foot had slipped off the footrest a couple of times and I felt something was wrong. I looked down once or twice and

HUTCHY: MIRACLE MAN

my concentration was wandering. I was running in fourth place and my foot kept slipping off. I could see I had oil on my boot and I am totally against racing round the TT with an oil leak, for obvious reasons. So I came into the pit and said the race is over. It's a shame it has ended like this, I said, but what can I do? The team examined the bike and said there is a bit of oil on my foot but it must have just been out of an overflow or something and there is no oil on the bike. The leak, they insisted, was not all over the bike so I could carry on. So get on with it, was their instruction. You'll be okay.

Thankfully, I left the pit. Before long the race was red-flagged following a huge crash involving Guy Martin. So I was never going to win it and I was anyway sure I would have broken down on that motorcycle as I was still convinced it was leaking oil. And that would have been the cruellest of endings to my dream of a clean sweep.

The race was to be restarted, however, and I was still in it, so I returned to the pits. I said to the team if the race is going to go again we need to get the problem fixed. They weren't allowed to touch the bike until half an hour before the restart and at the time the restart hadn't been announced so no one was allowed near the bike. Everyone was in a bit of panic about getting it ready and as soon as the restart was announced (which also gave us the news that Guy would be all right but had been taken to hospital), the team got my bike fixed. I just thought: it is meant to be. I am destined to

114

win today. And I am going for it. It was a countdown to TT history in the making.

It was a total fresh restart. I went off the start line like a man possessed, and I was fortunate that John McGuinness, a Senior specialist of the top rank and probably the biggest threat to my victory, broke down behind me and was out of the race.

I was leading the race anyway, and was determined that it should remain that way. And it did – I held on to first position from the start to the end. Obviously, it would have been even more satisfying if John had been standing on the podium on the step below me. But who knows, if he had kept going, he may have still beaten me. His breakdown and consequent non-finish had definitely made it easier for me. Not only did bad luck hit McGuinness – Cummins had a crash off the side of the mountain, when, thanks to John having to quit, he was up into second place. By the last lap I ended up with something like a 37-second lead, with Ryan Farquhar in second place and Bruce Anstey third, in an eventful and hard-run battle.

I can't begin to describe what it felt like to be so comfortably leading my fifth TT in a week with no real challengers looming and, therefore, not to have any pressure on me. It was the best feeling ever. The atmosphere was electric and I could almost feel it, and certainly see it in the fans' spectacular reaction every yard of the way to the chequered flag. Everybody was hanging off walls cheering, waving programmes and flags and T-shirts, and I just revelled in their reactions with a big smile under my helmet – it was so emotional round that lap. I shall never forget it as long as I live. And to be able to take it all in and, importantly and essentially, hold my concentration and keep on racing to hang on to my advantage was crucial. I just had to race in the fullest sense of the word right to the end. And it really couldn't have turned out any more perfect.

It is beyond one's wildest dreams. You think: it is a ridiculous notion that I could win five TTs, all the solo classes, against opposition as formidable as the winning and skilful likes of John McGuinness, Bruce Anstey, Michael Dunlop, Conor Cummins and James Hillier, and plenty of other star turns, in one week. Absolutely phenomenal. That fills me with a sense of pride. But you have to rein in that accelerating and fantastic feeling with your inner concerns and messages to yourself like: Hold on. I've got to be cautious here because I don't want to crash, collide with somebody, fall off or do something stupid. You have to get that balance right when faced with something so potentially historic. The feeling, I must confess, can be overwhelming. You still have to get to the end to be the winner.

Now, when I think back, it felt strange because it was so rewarding not only to have built up such an emphatic and considerable lead, but that I didn't have to try too hard and overstretch myself to the point of risk. I think I did 127 mph on the last lap – my slowest lap ever! I exaggerate, of course, but as I had been clocking 130-mph laps, it was comparatively slow.

Ted Macauley writes:

> I can remember going to the Isle of Man when to do
> 127 mph down the Sulby Straight was considered
> to be amazing. I must say I have enthused about the
> TT since my first ever visit in 1961 when its magic
> completely gripped me. People who have never been
> can't really grasp its attraction and it is very difficult
> to get the impression over to somebody. The closest
> I ever got to the inner sanctum of the TT and the
> nerve-racking sensation it gives to those close to the
> riders, relatives or friends, was when I took Mike
> [Hailwood] back in 1978 and for three hours sat
> in the stand watching his genius reappear. He was
> my best friend, he was thirty-nine, he had not raced
> anything for eleven years, he had a limp and a pot
> belly, and he said we are just going to play around,
> we are going for the game, no pressure. We shared
> a room, we drove up to the paddock in the massed
> traffic on the Saturday morning as, down purely to
> his comeback, the biggest crowd ever started to jam-
> pack the vantage points. And I said to him. 'You
> have been telling me lies, haven't you?' He said:

'What do you mean?' I said: 'You are going to try and win, aren't you?' He said: 'Too fucking right I am.' And that was it – all week long he was saying, I am just playing, you know. To get involved to that degree, to have that much concern for somebody and be that close to them, I know and appreciate just what it is like, not only to compete at TT but to be a TT winner and to do it half a dozen times or whatever. I must say, thinking about you, Hutchy, doing five – I find it unbelievable. Absolutely remarkable.

It did not stop there. I was on a roll and riding at the very peak of my form on motorcycles that met all the demands forced on them. The next big-time event for me was the following month's Ulster Grand Prix at Dundrod in Northern Ireland, a favourite hunting ground of mine where they really love their motorcycle racing and their heroes, the Dunlop family, Joey particularly, an absolute legend as a road racer. Ironically, my Irish trip didn't get off to the best start and I had to retire my Superbike from the warm-up Dundrod 150 meeting staged just a few days before the main Dundrod event, which meant I was lacking mileage on the Superbike.

Unpromising start notwithstanding, I won the Superstock, with Keith Amor and Ryan Farquhar coming second and third respectively, and went on to win the Supersport, with Keith Amor behind me, followed by Michael Dunlop. For the Superbike, in spite of the lack of mileage on my motorcycle, I took victory in the Superbike race, ahead of Bruce Anstey and Keith Amor. In the second Supersport race, to remind me that I was not invincible, I came second to Keith Amor's first place, with William Dunlop coming third; and in the second Superbike, I came second to Bruce Anstey, with Keith Amor coming third.

My final road race of the season was in the Scarborough Gold Cup at Oliver's Mount. And I won, so managing to end Guy Martin's winning streak there that had started in 2003. Not only that, I was first across the line in each of the two legs of the David Jefferies Cup for 600cc bikes.

But let me come back to my fairy-tale TT experience. The place was buzzing and really busy and already growing with vast numbers of fans; even though the TT is massive now, it was big then. I remember going for a night out and I just couldn't enjoy myself. There were that many people revelling that night we ended up getting a little cordoned-off area in one of the nightclubs in the casino, and it was weird. When you have gone through all that you just want to shut down and keep a low profile, relaxing and enjoying the company of your mates, but someone is putting a drink in your hand every few minutes, wanting to congratulate you and be part of your fun. And you end up tipsy as can be because you have been treated to a good a few pints. You finish up just all over the place and barely in control. Everybody wants to be with you. The only way to avoid it would be go back to your hotel and lock yourself in your room. And that's difficult because underneath you want to have a good time, celebrating whatever success you may have enjoyed. There is no answer, really, no solution. So you might as well let yourself be carried along.

When you are back in the privacy and solitude of your room it is impossible not to replay all the action and the high points and try to lull yourself off to some thoroughly deserved sleep and rest. But I still now mentally rave on about that week, plus the fact that I am never allowed to forget it whenever I find myself in the company of TT and bike race fanatics, which is often. Then I just couldn't believe it had happened. And right now, years on, I can recall the Isle of Man in 2010 as the best place I could possibly be.

And, no, even though I am often asked, I don't remember having any moments in 2010. I remember between the NW and that unforgettable TT, meeting up with the friends that I used to be on road bikes with – Craig, Matt and Steve – and having a pint at a pub and they were asking which event I thought I could win. I answered I think I can win all five races – but, really, I never meant it. I just knew that any one of my bikes was capable of winning and it would be up to me, and I was ready, willing and able to go for it.

It became a joke that the sidecar people must have been glad I didn't race in their class.

We had a show-off motor parade on the Promenade, where the organisers took all the TT winners from that week up and down the seaside track in front of thousands of cheering fans and for the first time ever there were only two of us, the sidecar winner and me: Austria's Klaus Klaffenböck triumphed in both sidecar races. Seven TTs . . . two winners.

BERNIE ECCLESTONE

Bernie Ecclestone, Formula One's renowned supremo, may be the power behind four-wheel grand prix racing's success story, but his fondness for the two-wheeled sport, especially the TT, is an everlasting passion.

Combined with his teenage business acumen which steered him towards running a thriving motorcycle spares business after the war, he ventured, though without success, onto two wheels before a brief encounter with car racing terminated by a crash.

'My utmost admiration is for those brave bikers who take on the TT,' he says. 'It is a great spectacle and the absolute test of a competitor's willingness, and downright ability, to give it a go.

'Over the many years the TT has been run there have been

some truly memorable moments and some really tragic ones, too. And, once in a while, there comes along an extra special and unique talent. And it has happened again in the skilful and committed form of Ian Hutchinson.

'What he achieved in that amazing haul of five wins inside one week [in 2010] was historically outstanding. Then to come back from his big crash and be a winner again is a tribute to his courage, typical of a man with a bond to the TT. Upcoming riders facing the Isle of Man's ultimate challenge would do well to read this revealing account of his ups and downs and his fightback on two wheels.'

CHAPTER 6

MONKEYS AND THE GRIM REAPER

Even now, years later, the memory of the horrific crash that could have finished my career and left me crippled for life fills me with horror. It was a total nightmare. So bloody scary.

It was the week after Scarborough. September 2010. Life could not get any better. I had won at the North West, topped all the races at the TT, won three races at the Ulster Grand Prix, taken the Scarborough Gold Cup – and everything was just perfect. I was in a really good place in life and in my career. I had bought my new house. I was earning the necessary money to renovate it, and everything was going perfectly, on circuit and off. The next race was a British Supersport Championship race at Silverstone, a far safer environment than the TT's constant dodginess. On the opening lap, in wet and slippery conditions – not my favourite, as I have made clear – a bunch of riders including me crashed out. At that point, my luck ran out.

You don't lie sprawled helplessly in the middle of the track with thirty motorcycles hurtling towards you in a cloud of spray and expect to get away with it. And I didn't. While I was still lying there I was clipped by one motorcycle before another one ran into me as they tried to make their way through the slippery haze and scattered motorcycles.

I remember the minute it happened.

I remember as I sat there on the track, still numb from shock, thinking, Why now, why now? After sticking my neck out, racing right on the limit on risky road tracks like the TT, the North West 200, Macau and others, here I am, badly hurt after a freak accident on a relatively safe and easy track like Silverstone. What rotten bloody irony.

I was sitting on the track with my bust left leg. The pain was excruciating. I looked down and it was awful. The lower part of my leg seemed to be hanging off, the bone had burst out of the back of my leathers. I tried to hold my leg up by the knee to keep the bone off the dirty track; the pain worsened, and – by the time the safety people got to me I was in so much agony I was begging for painkillers. But it's hard to gauge intense discomfort like I was in because your body takes over a little bit and allows you to accept the most ridiculous pain in the world.

The first-aid team got me to the medical centre where

they gave me ketamine, which plunged me into a state of dazed torpor and eased the pain for a bit. I felt like I had been lowered into a padded box and after a while I was airlifted by helicopter to hospital in Coventry. As the helicopter started up, the pain began to return, but I was still heavily sedated.

When I came round at the hospital there was this guy telling me my leg was dead – useless – and they were going to have to amputate it. And that awful announcement got me screaming and yelling that no matter what happened they should not take off my leg. I told them to fuck off, I needed it. I can remember the guy holding my foot up for me to see and saying: 'Look at it.' It had turned purple. I couldn't feel it. 'Your foot is dead. Look at it. We can't keep it.'

I pleaded hysterically with Clive Padgett's wife, who had accompanied me there, to insist that whatever happened, however bad it was, they must not amputate.

They told me they were taking me to the operating theatre, and I thought back to right after the crash, while I was on the track clutching my leg, how when I saw the state it was in I had feared the worst, and had had the scariest thoughts imaginable, that it was coming off. But then, as I lay there so helplessly the first-aider attending to me, no doubt trying to ease my fears and give me a confidence boost, had said: 'No. It'll be OK. If you had one of the cleanest breaks ever it would look like this so don't panic just yet because obviously if you break your leg it is going to bend in half and the bone

127

is going to come out no matter how bad or good it is.' I had tried not to be too afraid and to believe what the first-aid man was telling me. Now, at the hospital, desperately clutching at straws, I tried to believe those soothing words.

As I was being wheeled to surgery I was conscious but in a lot of pain and drifting in and out of awareness from the morphine they gave me. But in my lucid moments I continued begging them not to amputate. You can't be relaxed in such a scary situation. You just hope and think it is never going to happen to you and when it does you hope and pray it won't be you ever again. You just have to discover a way to get through the drama and the agony, both mentally and physically.

There were compound fractures to both bones that run down from the knee – the tibia, or shinbone, and the fibula, the slimmer calf bone. In the theatre the surgeon put an external bar bolted into my knee and my ankle to keep my leg straight again and to see if there was any blood supply. Three arteries, I learned later, feed blood to each foot – of those serving my left foot, two had been severed or crushed. One had survived. Just one, but at least there was a blood supply intact. The doctors left the wound wide open with blood streaming from it throughout Monday, Tuesday and Wednesday so they could monitor what was happening to my blood flow, before they even started to consider fixing the wrecked bones.

In the meantime, my sister had contacted my parents,

who were in Spain at the time, and told them what had happened, and they drove non-stop in their motorhome to the Coventry Hospital to be with me.

Then an absolutely superb orthopaedic expert surgeon called Matija Krkovic, a renowned specialist in upper and lower limb trauma, came to see me. A consultant at Addenbrooke's Hospital in Cambridge, he is a genius in complex reconstruction and he became my lifeline. He had been doing his rounds when he saw my X-ray on screen. When he introduced himself he said he wanted to be involved and he spent every minute he could from then on in working to save my leg. He did a pile of drawings showing me how he was going to do it by building a frame around the damage to piece it all together again. He, and later Mr David Watt, a very experienced and gifted plastic surgeon, between them definitely saved my career with a dedication to their work that to my mind, and eternal gratitude, is unparalleled.

There was still talk of amputating my foot as it was not receiving enough blood, which caused the skin to die, so I had to have loads of skin grafts. I had so much skin taken off that there was no natural coverage for the wide openly and extensively bared bone.

I was in hospital for about three weeks from the time of the accident and went through the first week off my head on morphine and not really knowing, or caring, what was going on, but having some really weird dreams and hallucinations. The most vivid was having a load of monkeys bounding about around my bed and all over the place. Then I was getting imaginary pictures from a TV that wasn't there. To me it was definitely there, on an angle bracket, and one of the monkeys, a little thing with a spirally tail, kept jumping on and off and on and off, and I could see the top two screws of the bracket were coming out. And the monkeys went on jumping on and off my bed . . . People in my dreams were bringing me cakes and biscuits and sweets which I never touched but which were all eaten by the monkeys, who were terrorising my room and leaving crumbs everywhere! But for some reason I had it in my head that they had to be there and were part of my treatment, so I never complained about them and let them get on with their crazy antics jumping on and off my bed. I can remember finally buzzing the nurse who was caring for me saying I'd had enough of the chimps and could she get rid of them? She must have thought I was a head case and asked me what I was going on about. Then she told me it must be the morphine I was on and not to worry. They were not real, just opiate-induced wild imaginings.

I have seen scores of X-rays and pictures of the original injury, pinned, stapled strapped, plastered, bloody, unsightly and downright horrible to look at. So I won't go into too much of the gory detail. I was sent home with a skin graft on the back of my leg where the bone had come out, and I was thinking, Three months and I'll be good to go again. But after a couple of weeks the injury started playing up again, so I had to go into my local hospital for more treatment. The skin grafted onto my leg was dying because of an inadequate blood supply so the dark threat of amputation remained. I came out of the operating theatre with bone and ligaments entirely exposed, and the medical team saying they obviously could not leave my leg as it was and the only recourse seemed to be amputation.

I insisted that having gone through so much I just could not let them take my leg off and pleaded with them that there must be something they could do. It was my immense good fortune that the distinguished plastic surgeon David Watt was based at Bradford and he came to see me. I explained that I was a professional biker, it was my life, my all, and I needed my leg. He said he would give it a go and that the team would do all they could to save my leg and my career. A twelve-hour operation was the start of a marathon of visits to intensive care and the operating theatre. Another skin graft failed to work, and the following morning the surgeon took me back into the theatre to see what he could do. My parents were at the hospital and were being updated every step of the way, and they were warned that given the extent of the problem, my leg might have to be amputated after all. No alternative. Mercifully, I was under anaesthetic during all this. Eventually, the surgeon told my parents they could go home, that he was going to keep trying and would be in touch. I was still out cold – had been since 11 a.m. – but they knew that I had secured the surgeon's assurance that he would not amputate without talking to me first, so they left the hospital.

At 8 p.m. the surgeon phoned Dad from the theatre with what he suggested could be a solution. And Dad agreed that he should give it a go. So they took a massive patch of skin off my back where the blood vessels are supposedly better, a risky job, to patch up the damaged leg. I woke up in intensive care after a sixteen-hour operation, cut all over, my face so puffed up with the fluids they had pumped into me that I could barely open my eyes, and with machines bleeping all around me, and a nurse by my bedside. I had no idea then I was in intensive care until she told me. Drugged up as I was, I didn't know what she meant. I just presumed I had died and had been taken away on a spaceship! I was pissed off because I still had a bloody frame on my leg and I thought that if I am a goner everything should be brand new, a re-start on my body parts. The morphine effects were really weird. People who do that stuff for fun and excitement must be nuts.

I had a week of darkness and despair, the worst possible feelings. I'd had two back-to-back operations, one of twelve hours, the second lasting sixteen hours, and then had been stuffed with painkillers. Every time I closed my eyes the wind whistled through intensive care in my imagination and the Grim Reaper kept appearing. So graphically, I shouted at the nurse to send him away. And I kept asking her: am I going to die? And because of the skin grafts on my back, the agonising pain, and the awkward way I was propped up in bed with pillows supporting my leg, I was on another planet. I bent forward and felt something hot running down my back – soon I was sitting in a pool of blood. For the operation I'd been given heparin to thin the blood so now the blood just flowed and flowed from all the cuts in my back. As the doctors worked to make the blood clot I just thought I was going to bleed to death. I was at the lowest ebb and honestly thought I was going to die. And that was the only point I would ever have agreed on an amputation, I was in such pain and so distressed. But they told me not to panic, and assured me things were progressing, and eventually the blood began to clot. I was so drugged up I could not talk without weeping. I had to rehearse talking before I could dare call anybody on the phone. But that, I believe, is as bad as it got. From then on in it was a case of operation after operation to get the grafts and the wrecked bones to heal.

I came out on crutches and not once allowed my leg to be in contact with the floor for five or six months. Then after about seven or eight months I started walking without the crutches. I still had the frame on my leg and then, exactly a year on from my accident, it was taken off. The leg will always give me some discomfort. My ankle just does not work: I can just stand on it – and that's that. Nothing that puts it under any undue strain. Ironically, even if the leg was 100 per cent perfect I don't think it would make any difference to my lap times. In the darkest of my dark moments, and there were plenty, I was not thinking only about racing, I was concerned about saving my leg. But, when it looked as though I wasn't after all going to lose it, my only thoughts were about getting back on a bike and racing again as hard as I ever had, and taking the same chances that had become such a crucial part of my existence. Which was why, while I was still in intensive care and having difficulty even controlling my voice, drugged up as I was, I spoke to Shaun Muir, and somehow clinched a deal to a ride for Swan Yamaha in 2011, and was all set to spearhead the fiftieth anniversary of Yamaha's road racing campaign.

During my convalescence after the trauma of the setback I think it would have been impossible for anybody to believe and have full enough faith in me to reckon me as a comeback success story. But I think I was fortunate that, because I had won five TTs in one week just before the mishap, team bosses and sponsors still thought they'd have something to gain by running me and still had some confidence in my ability. But sad truth as it was, just as I was getting on top of my game, I lost four years through being run over and the aftermath of the necessary repair jobs. I was forced out of the remaining British Championship rounds, of course, but finished tenth in the standings. Out, too, went the Macau event. I was determined to be ready, willing and able for the start of the 2011 short circuit season, but in the event that was a non-goer as well. And I had to miss both the North West 200 and the TT.

When I told my dad I'd signed to ride again he advised me that it was not the right time to tell my very concerned and upset mum that I was going back to racing. So she knew nothing of my intentions for quite a while. In any case, continuous physical hitches through the ongoing effects of the damage to my leg ruled me out of the TT.

Withdrawing from the TT was tough but it was the right decision, made on the advice of my surgeon, who was even so very encouraging, telling the press that my progress was 'setting new standards in orthopaedic trauma surgery. To get as close as he has to competing at the TT Races less than a year after his accident at Silverstone is nothing less than remarkable and I am sure he will win many more races in future.' And although I was letting him down, Shaun Muir was also supportive, saying, 'Everyone at Yamaha is really disappointed for Ian who has worked so hard to get back to fitness but . . . we look forward to seeing him return to the TT Races in 2012.' I rode several exhibition laps around the Mountain course with the frame still on my leg and was touched and heartened by the fantastic acclaim of the fans. That response and recognition gave my determination an unforgettable boost to get back into full flow as soon as I could. And I was up for it. By the end of the year I was begging Shaun to let me ride the bike once the frame was off my leg.

I could not change gear because I couldn't lift my left foot: it was and is useless. During the year the frame was still on my leg, I'd been seeing Mr Krkovic, the surgeon who had been and still was working tirelessly to fix my bones, and I had been badgering him about my foot. But he said the tendon had been severed and I would never be able to use it to change gear. Why, he asked, couldn't I use my right foot? This was clearly a mad notion. As I said in an interview with the journalist Oli Rushby for an article for Bennetts, 'This was coming from someone who is obviously very good at being a surgeon but not so good at racing a motorbike, so I told him he had no idea what it'd be like to try and change gear with your right foot!'

I had a right-side gear shift fitted on a Swan Yamaha.

I did a track day at Cadwell for Shaun Muir, my first experience of riding a racing bike with a right-side gear shift. I got a few neutrals but generally it went OK. So much so I pleaded with Sean to let me race the bike. And he consented. It was a slow and patient build-up, with the result I did manage, later in the year, a return at the Macau Grand Prix, a really demanding circuit and a tough test, and I got the Swan Yamaha home in third place after qualifying on the front row and being in the lead for the opening two and a half laps. I can't begin to explain what an amazing lift that gave my confidence and my ongoing eagerness to get back into the swing of full-time racing at the highest level as soon as my wounds would let me . . . and I had mastered the new gear change system. I just did as much riding as I could as soon as I was fit enough to get on a motorcycle –

teaching on special track days or going out to Spain to put some riding time in there, as I had done earlier in the year. It was all about ensuring I was comfortable again and building my self-confidence, as well as getting used to the changed gear shift and to using a thumb-operated rear brake. It was essential that I should put in as much time as possible on a motorcycle on an extremely long road to recovery. The frustration can be overwhelming, but patience and common sense in such perilous conditions, when anything can go wrong so easily, have to be paramount.

ROGER BURNETT

Roger Burnett, a Senior TT winner himself in 1986 and World Superbike champion James Toseland's manager, now the owner and developer of a very posh golf club not far from his home on the east coast near Grimsby, is a personality I have long admired for his qualities as both a man and a superb and stylish racer in his heyday, winning a British championship. Which is why I find his remarks about me both flattering and encouraging.

Roger, a master of control and cool thinking, crucial attributes when you are taking on the TT's plentiful problems, won his race in a week of awful weather when, tragically, four other guys were killed racing there. I was fascinated to hear his acutely worked-out system to underpin his chances of victory. He offers it as a tip: 'I believe the reason for my win in 1986 was my strategy when my bike was airborne.

'What I did when I was in the air and which my teammate then, Roger Marshall, did not do, was to neutralise the throttle in mid-flight so that when the rear wheel hits the ground again it is not spinning faster than it should be, which could cause trouble.

'If you do keep the throttle open the tarmac will slow down the engine as the back wheel hits the track. This puts a strain on the chain and I avoided all that threat of breakage which helped me in part on my way to victory. In very stark contrast Roger, who didn't follow my system, spent more time in the pits than I did. And I got away with it. Clever me!

'I don't know whether Hutchy does what I discovered was a distinct benefit in reducing any risk, but whatever he does – or did with his five fabulous wins in one week – he is on the right track.

'He is without a shadow of doubt an incredibly special rider of supreme talent, in the same mould as the truly unforgettable Steve Hislop, who won eleven TTs as well as the British Superbike championships in 1995 and 2005, plus the 250cc title in 1990. He was only forty-one when he died in a helicopter crash in 2003 when he was piloting. The vividness of his ability was his striking legacy. A great and modest guy, too.

'I honestly believe Hutchy is on a par with Hislop's gift as a goer of hard-to-beat quality. To win five TTs in one week is both a credit to him and the wonderfully enthusiastic Padgett team that backed him to such glory.

'Modern-day bikes are very individual, so to swap machinery from class to class, with all the differing subtleties and complications involved, and win on them all is a big test of ability and know-how and an extremely special achievement.

'Hutchy is one of life's real and genuine gentlemen, a quietly spoken guy who lets his motorbike-racing skill do the talking for him.

'Not too many riders come back from a life- and career-threatening crash to train and commit themselves back to a situation where they have to swap gear-change feet and still win so convincingly under the most dangerous circumstances, when you do not get a second chance in the most dodgy of wheel-to-wheel confrontations.

'But that is just Hutchy. And to my unashamedly admiring mind that is amazing beyond anybody's wildest imaginings, and I firmly believe he could go on to be the most successful Isle of Man TT rider of all time.'

CHAPTER 7

ANOTHER BREAK

Over a year after the crash my leg was still very weak. After Macau, as part of my getting-fit regime, I went to Australia for five weeks with Glen Richards to do some training and cycling and try to get some strength back in my leg. When I came back from there I went, in February, to the 2012 Carole Nash MCN Motorcycle Show at Excel in London to do some shows on little kids' bikes. But as I was rehearsing for the show on an off-roader I slid off, twisted my leg awkwardly and did my foot no good again. Another bloody total disaster! I'd done a deal with Shaun again. I had messed him about the first year. The second year, while I was in Australia, he had made me an offer to do British Superbikes for 2012 as Tommy Hill's teammate. My dream was all back in place and I was going to be riding for

Yamaha at the TT in 2012 – then this freak crash happened and I just thought: I can't let Shaun down again. I rang my surgeon and said I've broken my leg again and told him I was coming to see him right away. And I drove straight up to Coventry.

I wouldn't let anyone else look at my leg. I went straight to see him, and he said, 'It's a really straightforward fracture, low energy, but I need to put a frame on your leg again. I have no idea why it's broken – I don't understand, it's fresh, it's not where the old injury was.'

Same leg but not where the mega problem had been. He put a frame on my leg and said that at best it would take three months for it to heal, which would be just two weeks before the North West 200. So I told Shaun and the Yamaha team I would be ready for the NW and the TT. Obviously, I wouldn't be doing British Superbikes. Then I just had everything in my mind focused on getting race ready. I kept training through it all, went to the gym, did everything I could, exercising with a frame on my leg to get this new injury healed. The surgeon had said to leave it until the end of April. 'We don't want to keep X-raying it,' he said, 'That's no good for healing. Come back then and hopefully I can take the frame off.' So I went to see him at the end of April, with two weeks to go before the NW 200. I had told Yamaha I would be ready for the race.

The doctor X-rayed my leg and came out and floored me with the rotten news that the bone was infected and

'It's not healing at all. I'm going to have to cut out five or six inches of bone completely and start a bone transplant, which is going to take about eighteen months.' I said, 'There is absolutely no way that can happen. I am racing at the NW in two weeks and then the TT.' He said: 'Well, your leg is still broken, this is obviously why it is a problem now. We understand that the bone was infected inside and was weak and snapped where it was infected. Because it's broken the infection has started to come out and started to eat into you.' There were big holes in my leg through my skin where it was eating out, but I said: 'Well, I still need to race at the NW in two weeks and then the TT. After those, you can do whatever you want. Can you take the frame off? How can I race? Will it make it any worse if I ride on it?' He told me if I crashed it would probably rip my leg clean off. And I replied that if I fell off at the TT my leg would be the least of my worries. I said I needed the frame taken off and someone to make me a really light cast to hold the leg together.

He took the frame off that day and had a cast made, but it was clearly way too big for me to be able to get my leathers on. I then took a crazy course of action. I went home and rang up a local company that makes carbon fibre exhaust pipes and asked if I could buy some carbon fibre off them. I drove over there and bought the carbon fibre and resin. When I got back home I removed the cast and made my own from carbon fibre, much thinner – I had made a cut down the back of the old cast so that I could take it on and off to have a bath. When the cast was off I couldn't walk on my leg. Now, with it off, I wrapped my leg in cling film and then put this carbon matting around it and pasted the resin on. What I didn't know is that it heats up to about 100 degrees Celsius as it sets, so it was burning my leg but I had to put up with it as I wanted it to set hard. Once my cast was solid, I taped it up the back so it would be secure. Then I could walk.

The next step was to try to get through the medical at Oulton Park. I went there and told the medics that I had made the cast simply to protect my leg (leaving out the fact that I couldn't stand up without it as my leg was broken) and I assured them it was all good: I just didn't want anyone banging into me before the NW and TT. Somehow, I managed to get safely through my check-up and race at the NW. I came tenth in the first Supersport race, thirteenth in the first Superbike race and seventh in the second Superbike, I was encouraged and went on and did the TT.

In the opening Superbike race, I took eighth place, with my old friends and rivals John McGuinness, Cameron Donald and Bruce Anstey on the podium in that order. In the Supersport first race, I came ninth, with Bruce Anstey taking first place, followed by Cameron Donald and then William Dunlop. In the Superstock race, I was eleventh, with John McGuinness taking first, Michael Dunlop second and Ryan Farquhar third. The last race I rode in was the second Supersport, where I came sixth, with Michael Dunlop first,

Cameron Donald second and Ryan Farquhar third. The rest of the TT did not happen – for the first time in its history its races had to be cancelled because of the weather.

After the TT I had to go straight into the operating theatre. There was to be no Ulster Grand Prix for me that year. It was frustrating, but at least I had my three top-ten finishes in the TT as proof that I could still race a motorcycle. Once again, Shaun Muir was supportive, saying: 'It's a huge disappointment for Ian and the team, but we have to make sure he is medically well and we will support him all the way through this setback.'

It felt like I was going through the first leg-break all over again. Just before the TT, the surgeon had told me that he was just starting a similar procedure on someone, so now I asked how it was going with the other guy, and he said not to worry about him, he was a totally different case, and that he and his team were ready to start my process. I said, 'Yes . . . but what's happening with him?' 'Do not ask,' he said, but then went on: 'Well, we've amputated his leg.' Shit! But then he said to me: 'You're a totally different case. He wouldn't go through what he needed to go through, and he couldn't face the time and the pain it was going to involve. He didn't want to keep his leg.' Blimey . . . I asked the doctor if it was because the leg didn't work, and he answered that the guy had said it was because he was prepared to go through with the amputation. So I responded, Right . . . Okay . . .

They broke my leg just below the knee to cut the infected bone out of my leg. They chopped out six inches of tibia where it was infected either side of the second injury. Then came the bone transplant.

After the surgery, a frame was fitted to my leg, with three hand nuts on it that I had to turn every six hours of the day – 6 a.m., midday, 6 p.m. and midnight – I had to turn them ¼mm just to pull the bone through the inside of my leg and also shorten the lower part of the leg so that it would join up quicker. That was the worst. I did not touch my left foot to the floor for eleven months, and for a long time, the leg was three inches shorter than it had been, just dangling in the breeze. It took until the following July before I was able to dare press my foot on the floor. I went on a recuperation trip to Madeira and spent a lot of time walking up and down in the sea, and swimming. And that got me back on my feet, literally. I built my strength back, too, and then I started the process of trying to persuade Shaun to let me go to race the 2013 Macau Motorcycle Grand Prix. I assured him my frame would be off by the end of September. I desperately wanted to race. He thought I was crazy and didn't want me to go. On 26 September I had my thirtieth and hopefully last operation. I was all set to go. Then I heard that Shaun had missed the deadline for the Macau entries by one day, and I didn't have a chance of a ride.

I went absolutely crazy at Shaun because Macau had been my main focus to keep me going. I had genuinely believed I could go and win Macau, which would make everyone realise that I could do the TT again. He had not entered me! I had been relying on him to do so. No other team would believe I could come back and I had to prove myself on this bike – to prove that I could ride for anybody. So I created a massive fuss about not getting entered. Eventually a rider dropped out, and I reckoned this was my golden opportunity. Even so, the organisers still hummed and hawed about whether to let me go or not, because I hadn't ridden for so long – I hadn't ridden for a year and a half. It just took so much effort to get myself out there with the team and all the setbacks. And obviously I had lied to the medical team before so they were unsure whether I was fit to go or not. But anyway, it all happened and I got the frame off my leg. I borrowed a Superstock bike off the team, had it shipped to Spain, where I spent four days riding it at Almeria.

In November I went out to Macau for the forty-seventh motorcycle Grand Prix around the 3.8-mile (6.2 km) Guia circuit, riding Shaun's Milwaukee Yamaha. I struggled a little bit in the first session, I think I was sixth or seventh, but did better in the second session, then in final qualifying we made a last-minute change and I went out and set pole position for the race. I had left the pit lane when apparently Michael Rutter, the most successful winner ever there, happened to see my pole position time. He was surprised, I'll bet. I had outqualified him and that made me believe I had got the better of him and that I could win this race.

I had a bit of a crap start and dropped back to fourth place, but then got into my rhythm and came through into third, then second and I was on the back of Rutter. I really wanted just to run most of the race behind him because I hadn't raced for so long and I just wanted to follow him. But I kept seeing the lap times weren't that strong and I know what Michael is like. He is very clever at working out what he needs to do and then acting accordingly. I thought he was probably trying to hold the pace up so he could go for it at the end. But I was ready to go. I fully believed that I was the strongest man out there and that I could win this race. So I passed him and set off and pulled out a gap straight away. I opened up the advantage to about three or four seconds and then came across some backmarkers. But I just coolly carved my way through them. I was like a man possessed. I built a seven-second lead. And top guys and proven winners like John McGuinness and Gary Johnson, as well as Michael, were behind me. I thought: I have got this all wrapped up now, with just two laps to go. And then on lap 12 the red flag came out. One of the other racers had highsided – fortunately he was not badly hurt, but it was enough to bring the race to an end.

A big shame, that. But, as the race was 75 per cent through its scheduled course, the officials declared it complete. So I had won. I would have liked to have gone to the end, the full distance, to win it. And I'm sure Michael Rutter, Gary

Johnson (third) and John McGuinness (fourth) were also sorry the race came to an early end. But, for me, the real treat and benefit was that my competitors got the message that I was back in the hunt – big time. That race was so fantastically important in the re-making of me on my way back to where I am right now.

So having sat out eighteen months before coming back at the end of 2013 to win in Macau, I could not wait to get going in 2014 with Milwaukee Yamaha. Once again Shaun Muir had put his full belief in me and had a second team built around me for British Superbikes, so with the main team for the road race, things were back on track, or so I thought. But the season turned out to be on a par with my year with AIM Yamaha in 2008 – a total disaster . . .

CHAPTER 8

2014: A SEASON TO FORGET

After the success in Macau, I was looking forward to getting back to a full programme of racing the following year. The 2014 season started off as usual with testing out in Spain. The kind of 'B' team to the Milwaukee Yamaha outfit that Shaun Muir set up for me was run in the livery of FFX, another sponsor who came on board for my first attempt at a season in British Superbikes. The bike was similar to the one on which I had won in Macau, but with the less sophisticated Motec-controlled electronics, which were a requirement of the rules in BSB. I did, however, get my own crew chief, Chris Anderson, who became a great friend. He remains someone whom I trust and upon whom I continue to rely.

Testing went really well in Spain, and I came back and got stuck into the racing. It was tough and, as I expected, really hard even to finish in the points, but as the season went on the bike proved to be one that I just couldn't get on with. I had many crashes, which is unusual for me, and my results never really improved. Far worse for me, however, was that when I switched back to the main team I also struggled.

During the winter the race organisers had decided to change the rules about the electronics allowed on Superbikes at the TT for 2014. This meant that, after months of battles between them and the team, we had to take off all the kit that I had won with in Macau and start again with the spec we were using in BSB. Along with this, the so-called super-special 600cc Yamaha R6 that the team were building for me wasn't finished until a week before the North West 200 in May, so I never got to test it.

In fact, the NW 200 marked the beginning of the end of the relationship between me and the Milwaukee Yamaha team. We got out to Ireland, but to be honest, I might as well have stayed at home. Having stated in the winter my preference about who I wanted in my team for the road-race meetings, I learnt that they were to be working with the team's other rider, Josh Brookes. I found the bikes were problematic throughout practice, and I came off the 600 exiting Mill Road Roundabout, where I slid up the road with the bike on top of my hand, taking off all the skin and breaking my little finger.

I thought, This is my first real year back racing and I'm already in hospital, only two weeks before the TT! The accident caused friction between everyone including my mum, who found that she could no longer cope with the risks involved. This was to be the last race she ever came to.

I sat down with Shaun before the TT and we went through what had to change to salvage at least a podium from the TT. For me, however, the 2014 TT was a complete and utter disaster. The following year was to prove to be a different story.

I regret that, out of sheer frustration, I did act irresponsibly towards the end of the fortnight, on one occasion having continued to ride the superbike back to the paddock, including through a wooded area, after its engine had blown up. I have to admit, too, to kicking my 600 as I threw it up against a wall, having broken down for about the fourth time, on this occasion only a few miles into the race. So it was probably not a great surprise when, in August, less than two months after the TT, Team Milwaukee Yamaha and I parted company.

With the TT out of the way – and best forgotten, to my mind – I did some track days and a round of National Superstock at Silverstone, which was terrible as I struggled my way to twentieth place. Macau was also an uphill struggle and I eventually overshot a corner during the race and retired.

Some time earlier, I had agreed to ride for PBM the following year, using their bikes for some of the TT and other races. By now, however, I knew that Paul Bird was having second thoughts about running me for 2015, so I went to see him and explained that I needed time on the bike to get my confidence back. With some persuasion from Blandy – Stuart Bland, the PBM team co-ordinator – Paul kept me on and agreed to give me what I needed.

I was grateful for his faith in me, and determined to live up to my side of the bargain. But whatever our hopes for the new season, I don't think that either he or I could ever have envisaged just what rewards our association would bring.

STUART BLAND

I first met Ian in the scrutineering bay at Thruxton in 2005. He had just had a huge crash and snapped his Fireblade in half. John McGuinness, who I had worked with for many years, had shown an interest in Ian and I joined in the conversation. Over the year Ian joined in with our gang and came on some of our trail-riding trips and nights out and became a good friend. Contrary to many people's first impression of Ian being a quiet, shy, sensible chap, this could not be further from the truth.

On our nights out he would always be the one doing something daft and being the life and soul of the party. Also on our trail-riding trips, usually to the Isle of Man, he would be the one doing one-handed wheelies past a car on the road or hitting the deepest bog flat out and having a huge crash.

In 2006 Ian's riding skill really improved and for the end of season for the Macau GP Paul Bird asked Ian to ride the Stobart Honda BSB bike. He did really well despite a crash in practice in which he did a double somersault over the crash barrier and walked back to the pits unharmed. He finished third on only, from memory, his second visit.

The goings-on away from the racing are now legendary, with him at the centre as usual, including setting fire extinguishers off in nightclubs, coming back to the hotel at seven in the morning completely paralytic at breakfast, throwing McGuinness's bed out of the window and all sorts of wild stuff. The 'headmaster' of the trip, Mike Trimby, used to tell everybody to calm down every now and again, while laughing at the same time.

Ian rode for Paul Bird Motorsport again at Macau in 2007 and 2009 and 2014 and 2015 but never rode full time until he was sacked by Yamaha towards the end of 2014. Ian had always been a friend of the PBM team and Paul Bird offered to put him on a Superstock bike for the last three races with a plan to do the roads the following year. This went okay – but the results weren't great as his confidence was completely gone. But he got used to the Kawasaki ZX-10 and Paul agreed to put a programme together with him for 2015.

The plan was to do an extensive testing programme with mainly the Superbike and then do the first three British Superbike races. And this went perfectly and his confidence and self-belief slowly returned.

The first three BSB races went okay, nothing spectacular but good solid results and most importantly his times were usually within one second of Shakey (Shane Byrne), his teammate.

We arrived at the North West 200 and Paul Bird was confident that Ian would do well and would have been happy with top five. But from the first lap of race we knew we were in with a good chance of victory in all the races.

When we arrived at the TT the team was really behind him and his confidence was sky high, but for a few small problems in the Superbike races it could have been five in a week again with us and he was clearly the top rider at the great festival. As it was he managed three wins, the Monster Energy Supersport Class, races one and two, and another victory in the RL360 Superstock race.

We had travelled to the island from Liverpool on the jet boat and nobody even asked for his autograph. Regular TT fans had written him off. In complete contrast, on the boat on the way home he was mobbed. What a difference a week makes. But what else could you expect from a gifted talent like Hutchy, who just does not know how to give up, even against the biggest and most formidable odds on track or, as he has shown, off it and in private when your resilience is being put to the full test.

CHAPTER 9

TREBLE VICTORY: TT 2015

To have won all five solo races at the TT against talented and highly experienced, top-line opposition of the most determined type, as I did in 2010, is an achievement that I can still scarcely credit. Even now, I still have to pinch myself to believe it all happened . . . that I became a history-maker, my name mentioned with TT legends and world champions like Mike Hailwood, Geoff Duke, Stanley Woods and Joey Dunlop, all winners on the world's most challenging road-race circuit. Incredible.

So it didn't really seem possible that I might get close to that towering level ever again. And yet my winning return to the island in 2015, after my appalling injuries, is the stuff of fairy tales. When you emerge strongly, triumphantly, from bleak adversity, and escape the clutches of self-pity and doubt to regain confidence and ability, the feeling of inner satisfaction is almost immeasurable. The intervening years, between my accident in 2010 and my return to winning and record-breaking form five long and agonising years later, were the most frustrating times of my life.

The appreciation shown so spectacularly and noisily by the fans that June week in 2015 – and ever since, really – was, and still is, an extra special sensation. To recover the magic of my success at the TT that year, I can do no better than quote the eyewitness reports of John Watterson, nowadays Sports Editor of Isle of Man Newspapers, and then the main writer on *TT News*, a special edition recording the events in detail. Under the headline 'The Bingley Bullet is Back', Watterson wrote:

Ian Hutchinson, the Bingley Bullet is back. And with a vengeance.

The thirty-five-year-old, who very nearly lost his left leg following an accident at Silverstone in 2010, announced his return with a heroic win in Monday evening's four-lap Supersport 1 race.

After a near-five year battle back to fitness, and as many as thirty different operations, an emotional Hutchy was initially unable to speak in the post-race press conference, but he eventually regained his composure to admit that his victory was very special.

'People have been great and I am really grateful

for all of the support I have had over the past five years. I was originally down to ride a red bike, the MV Agusta, but we made a late change to a Yamaha. Keith Flint [front man for The Prodigy] and the team at Traction Control put together a package for me and, despite only completing three laps in practice, the bike was an absolute dream to ride. It was as if I was delivering pizzas!

'Starting number 9 was not ideal. Some people obviously thought I wouldn't be able to live with the pace up front so I got dropped down the starting order. Guy Martin held me up a bit early on, but I eventually got clear and was able to up my pace.

'I missed a pit board at Ballaugh on lap one and it was a fair old chunk of time round to Ballacraine for my next one.'

Regarding the huge reception he received in the winners' enclosure, Hutchinson responded, 'I was always going to hear it again one day. Setting the pole in qualifying on the big bike put a lot of pressure on me for the Superbike race, but I was a lot better today and I soon settled down. I was cruising.

'Keith Flint willed me to do it. It is a pity he was not here today to see this, but he will be made up. He is coming tomorrow (Tuesday). He was gigging at the Isle of Wight over the weekend and then in Germany to get the cash for this TT.'

Hutchinson, the record five-times winner in 2010, was not to be denied and he punched the air in delight as he crossed the finish line to firmly announce his comeback and claim his ninth TT win. He received one of the loudest receptions in TT history when he flicked his Yamaha right into the winners' enclosure. And even his closest rivals were full of praise for the gently spoken Yorkshireman, who for a couple of years was the forgotten star of the TT.

'He deserves it,' said a sporting Anstey, the runner-up, 'he rode very well. Every time I pushed he pushed even harder. I made a couple of mistakes, but I went as hard as I could. It was windy in places and I hit the kerb at the top of Bray Hill on the opening lap . . . my arms and legs were flailing around and it took me a lap to settle down. I pitched in a 127 mph lap to see if I could break him.'

Third-placed Gary Johnson commented: 'I am really happy for Ian. I saw the speed and the momentum he was carrying when he passed me and I thought: fair play to you, mate!

'I was in hospital last year after coming off in the Superstock race, but my injuries were nothing like as serious as those Hutchy suffered. I didn't know if he could get through this TT – but he has. And superbly.'

'And it was not too long before Hutchy was at it again,' writes Ted Macauley, 'he roared back to another level of his best in the Superstock race when he had barely recovered from his classy show in Supersport 1.'

Again John Watterson recaptures the action under the *TT News* magazine headline: 'Hot Hutch Storms to Victory'. I can barely believe I am reading about myself! He wrote:

Less than eighteen hours after recording an emotional Supersport win, Ian Hutchinson added another fabulous victory in the RL360 Superstock event on Tuesday.

This race for him was in many ways an even more impressive feat as he beat Michael Dunlop into second place.

'In the four years I have been away from the top, Michael has been THE man around here,' said Hutchinson, who had been fighting to hold back the tears in the post-race press conference the previous evening.

'I knew Michael would make it a lot harder for me, so it is even more special beating him.'

Hutchy's PBM Kawasaki team boss, Paul Bird, admitted that the team's ace card had been deciding to change the rear wheel at the pit stop.

'It was a big ask beating the BMWs on the Kawasaki, so I knew we needed new tyres on the rear for the second half of the race,' said Bird, who has been away from the TT for the past decade while he chased the MotoGP and World Superbike dream.

Hutchinson admitted he had not been comfortable with the suggestion of changing wheels as it can be a scary exercise on a Superstock machine.

'They only told me this morning what they planned to do, but I wasn't altogether happy with it. I told the young mechanic, Sam, that I did not want to see my wheel nut rolling down the pit lane beside me.

'But he did an excellent job and there is no doubt that the new tyre gave me the edge in the closing stages. And it would have been hard work completing four laps on one tyre. My biggest fear was running out of fuel.

'The bike started running out of gas at the 32nd Milestone at the end of lap two, so I was passed by Guy Martin. After topping it up I knew that I had to go hard on lap three to get a decent advantage in case I had to free-wheel a bit on the final lap.

'It started to cut out at the Bungalow and I had to sit bolt upright slipstreaming behind John McGuinness to try and conserve more fuel. Every time I leaned the bike over I felt it holding back. It was a nightmare.

'Then at Bedstead it cut out altogether. I coasted into the corner and it ran wide onto the pavement, bumping it back down onto the road. Not ideal!'

The somewhat desperate fuel-conserving methods

worked and Hutchinson completed the final three-quarters of a mile okay to take his second chequered flag in as many days. And what is more, he smashed the old race record by a whole 32 seconds. Bizarrely, Michael Dunlop's lap record of 131.220 mph from 2013 remains intact.

One second and a half covered him [Dunlop], James Hillier and Hutchy at Glen Helen, with Mickey D a full 2 seconds clear at Ramsey from Hutchinson, with Hillier, third, 1.5 seconds down. Dunlop held the lead heading into the pits where the official time split was exactly two seconds.

Paul Bird's Motorsport team did an absolutely amazing job in the pits. Not only did they fill up the tank, they also changed the rear wheel and still grabbed a 3-second lead over Michael Dunlop at the same time.

The headlines were full of my comeback, and there were generous appraisals of my wins. And it didn't stop. Here, again, is another flattering write up by John Watterson in *TT News* under the banner 'Hutchy Clocks Up TT Win Number 11':

Such is the rediscovered fitness and form of Ian Hutchinson, that he described his winning ride in Wednesday's Supersport 2 race as more like a four-lap practice session.

Chalking up his third win in as many days, the 2010 history man was already eyeing up a possible fourth win in Friday's Senior and what would be an eleventh win overall.

His comeback is almost complete, but few truly thought he would ever stand on the podium again, never mind rattle up a hat-trick of amazing wins in one of the most remarkable stories in motorsport history.

The comeback hero said: 'I did my usual thing and kept it steady in the early stages and then gradually worked my way into the lead to build up a safe buffer. We left the bike as it was on Monday, but the team told me last night that they were going to put in another engine – and that got me a bit concerned. On lap three I started shifting up gears early to give it an easier time, but then my lead dropped down to 8 seconds so I had to up it again on the last lap. I am enjoying just being back.'

A final lap speed of 127.476 mph gave Hutchinson a winning margin of 14.82 seconds to snatch his eleventh TT win, putting him level with Phillip McCallen, Steve Hislop and Michael Dunlop – but he now has more 600cc class wins than anybody else.

Anstey commented: 'Hutchy smoked us all today. I was flat-out all the way and conditions were great, the best I have seen here for years. But I could not do anything about Ian. He is really on it.'

Third-placed Martin was also full of praise for the winner, saying, 'Ian is riding bloody well. I was with him for a while, but we hit some traffic and he got away. I rode my own race for a while until I caught up with Gary Johnson. It has not been the best of weeks for me, but it is not all doom and gloom and I am happy.'

Team boss Keith Flint hailed my double success on the Team Traction Control Yamaha R6. He had stepped in at the eleventh hour to fix me up with two Supersport rides. Afterwards he praised my effort as 'Unbelievable'. And he added: 'People have been coming here for twenty years and still not had a win, nothing to do with the riders, the mechanics or the team, it is just so hard to be a winner at the TT. To have been behind Ian in what he has achieved so brilliantly on what has been a moving and fantastic comeback has left me speechless.

'We always put a team out to be winners. We were not here just to take part – but you can never, ever count on the TT giving what you want in return for your effort. That's just the way it is. To be part of TT history has always been my dream, a lifelong ambition, then to get two wins in a week is amazing, absolutely amazing. I don't think that feeling is ever going to settle.'

From my own standpoint, the entire experience of my comeback was as emotional as can be, and to have returned to the top step of the podium after winning the Supersport opener, when the last time I had done so was five years earlier, is a sensation beyond description. I owe Yamaha: they have been behind me all the years I was trying to make a comeback after shattering my leg. I rode in 2012 and was not capable of any results – but they stood firmly behind me, and again in 2013. We had our problems, but they backed me through all the issues and setbacks.

I know how much Keith Flint loves the TT. So a week before the race, when my ride on the MV Agusta fell through, I asked them to come back to the island and they pulled a set-up together for me and arrived on Monday night with the bike coming on Tuesday. I managed to get in only three practice laps – and won! Fantastic! I only just missed out on Sunday's Superbike race, second to Bruce Anstey, after a real tough battle. But inside twenty-four hours I was back on the top step.

It was five years after the crash, an absolute torment of a barren spell. And what an unforgettable and welcome comeback that was to the top step of the grandstand podium, which across the years had welcomed so many TT heroes. And now television pundits, among many others, who had believed I would never race again were in open admiration that I was mentally, if not absolutely perfectly physically, up for a comeback, bigtime, around the Isle of Man's ultra-ultra-challenge. My time on the sidelines had been a real heartbreaker, and I reckon I had missed out on twenty potential wins in that period, given the way I was riding on my return. So it was just great to get back in 2015. Everything I had been through, the pain, the worry and the suffering, was suddenly a distant memory and I was a winner. Again.

'They should make a film about him. His return to racing from such a serious situation and such a real threat to his career has been fairy tale,' said 2003 WSB champion Neil Hodgson, 'I can't believe he did it.'

'And I could not agree more,' added twice British title-holder Jamie Whitham, 'it makes me proud to know him as well as I do.'

'I don't think any of us believed he would ever ride – never mind race – a bike competitively again,' said my old and fearsome rival Michael Rutter.

Sure, it was tough coming back, and you always think about accidents like mine, 'It will never happen to me.' Then it does and you say to yourself, 'It'll never happen again.' The lay-off time was all a blur. At first, when I got injured, I thought I'd be off for about three months. If I had known it was going to be three years I would probably not have been able to cope and go through with it. But I broke it down into stages, and refused to allow myself to fret about how long it would take for me to get going again and take up where I had been forced to leave off . . . as a winner.

When you suffer injuries like mine and are forced to undergo such extensive and seemingly endless treatment, you find you are scared of motorbikes. You don't want ever to go near one again. But it is a bit like a hangover when you swear you are never going to drink again. Then, when the hangover and the headaches and the sickness have gone, you are straight out boozing again. And here I am – back on the road, the one that really matters, having turned my nightmare into a dream.

The TT is one race on its own. Unique. You just have to look back, for when people have been successful in the past they normally continue to be so for a very long time. It is a race where so many things need to be just perfect. Nobody is ever going to come along and win five races in a week every year for the decade, but I hope I will be winning for a good while yet. And, I promise, giving it my all to repeat my historic 2010 breakthrough.

RICK BROADBENT

R ick Broadbent, a motorcycle-racing enthusiast and respected sports writer on *The Times*, a good friend of Ted Macauley's, asked me for an interview for his newspaper ahead of the 2016 TT, and later gave his permission for some of its use in my book. He captures the atmosphere and reflects my feelings excellently, and I am flattered by his assessment of my ability.

[Ian Hutchinson's] comeback to win three races at the TT last year was a physical and mental wake-up call to pampered egotism of sport. 'Jesus, it was some pain,' the 'Bingley Bullet' said of seeing his leg 'hanging off'. 'When they said they would have to amputate I said "F*** off, I need it . . ."' It is hard to judge pain because your body takes over a little bit and allows you to have the most ridiculous pain in the world.'

The TT is extraordinarily dangerous as motorcycles reach 200 mph on roads lined by trees, walls, pubs and houses. Calls to have road racing banned have increased in tandem with each fatality. Some struggle to justify the annual balancing of free will with the tragic inevitability, but it makes for astonishing personal challenges and jaw-dropping sport.

Hutchinson's odyssey led him to plumbing rare depths. The Yorkshireman remembers chatting to Conor Cummins, another top rider who crashed off the Mountain in 2010 and broke his back in five places and his arm in four, as well as fracturing his pelvis, bruising his lungs, breaking his collar bone and shattering his knee joint. Cummins admitted he hurtled over a dry stone wall and into depression, but he is a TT racer and will be racing again this year. 'We've had chats about stupid things,' said Hutchinson, 'the issues with painkilling drugs and multiple operations – you start hallucinating and have nightmares, get horrendous constipation; the spewing up when you come out of the theatre; you are so ill for someone who has just damaged a bone.'

This year [2016] Hutchinson's bikes for the five races include the Supersport Yamaha of a team fronted by Keith Flint, the lead singer of The Prodigy. He also says that he is proud to be riding for the old team of David Jefferies, the biggest name to be killed at the TT back in 2003. His team manager, Philip Neill, still does not attend the Thursday of practice week. After that accident, and the legal wrangle that followed, he asked himself whether it was worth it. 'There used to be far too many fatalities,' he said. 'That is not sustainable. That is not even sport.' He reasoned that a ban would force the sport underground and he might as well try to make it as safe as he could.

Hutchinson shrugs at the danger and says accidents to the top riders are few and far between. He also welcomes the increasing professionalism, which angers those for whom this is the last great bastion of Corinthian spirit. 'The more you ride here, the more you learn,' he said, 'you know where you can push hard and where it is not worth it. I am glad it is getting corporate, as long as the riders get something, because we are professionals. This is not club racing.'

There is a beauty in the bravery of the bereaved and desire is the heartbeat of the TT. Hutchinson, who says his parents refused to buy him a bike, was fastest in the first practice sessions and looks set to overcome his battered body again. Like it or not, on the Isle of Man, every parent, partner, mechanic, punter and racer is ready for the life-affirming thrill of dream-chasing.

HUTCHY: MIRACLE MAN

Rick Broadbent's graphic summation of the sport generally, and the TT in particular, the risks and the rewards, is the sort of realistic view we who are connected with the race, in whatever role, should take to heart.

CHAPTER 10

ANOTHER THRILLER OF A WEEK: TT 2016

When the 2016 TT loomed, my anticipation and excitement were as strong as they had been before my first ever taste of the track and its formidable challenge, when I was a novice filled with ambition to master its endless vagaries. Yes, of course, by 2016 I had been a winner in the island many times, headlined by my five-in-a-week romp into the record books in 2010. But even so, every time I race the place I feel a renewed need to be the winner, the record-breaker, the rider remembered for his dash and daring. Nothing, therefore, had changed: my attitude was a carefully studied one of anticipation without cockiness, as down to earth as I could be. This time I was just three wins short of standing level with one of the all-time greats of the TT, Mike Hailwood, fourteen times a winner there, an eternal hero not only to TT fans but to bike race followers the world over.

By now I was under new guidance in the shape of Philip Neill, who had been running the TAS (Temple Auto Salvage) team with his dad Hector for sixteen years. But Hector's pedigree as a team boss went back to the 1970s when he supported Joey Dunlop, the Northern Irish genius who won twenty-six TTs and was on the podium forty times, as well as TT hotshots Johnny Rea and Steven Cull under his own team banner. The father and son had fifteen TT wins on their list – but had not won in the island for eight frustrating years. In fact, the Northern Ireland-based outfit had last sampled TT glory when Cameron Donald snatched a stock race win on his Relentless Suzuki in 2008. By 2016, however, they were sponsored by Tyco and running BMWs.

Ahead of our tie-up and the TT Philip said: 'TT wins are getting harder to come by. And the less you have something the more you want it. We have been lucky to have had fifteen victories – but recently they have been few and far between. However, we are one of the teams that would still be at the TT even without the incentive of a commercial platform. We have been going there since the days when there were not those commercial opportunities, so it is clearly a passion thing for us. It is in our DNA.

'So, as a team still fired by ambition and an eagerness to win, we want a TT first-placer more than ever. The hype that is built up around the race worldwide is massive. And to have a win under that spotlight would be a joy beyond measure.'

That was the boss's absolute dream and it was in my hands to try my best to realise it. And I did! I rode under the number 4, coincidentally the same as my start plate in 2010, that fantastic and notable week in June. In Monday afternoon's Superstock race, from a standing start, I set the standard with a great opening lap of 133.098 mph, which was just 0.510 seconds off the 17-minute-lap barrier and only 2.256 seconds down on Michael Dunlop's outright lap record set on his Superbike spec BMW S1000RR in the previous Saturday's race, when he pushed me and my Tyco BMW into second place. That time virtually sealed the race in my favour from lap one.

I had an inkling that it was going to be impressive, having done a lap of 132.8 mph in Friday's practice. I knew I could top even 133 mph if I had to, so I was well in control. When Dunlop retired his BMW with a broken gear lever at the end of lap one I was 16 seconds in the lead. It was my thirteenth TT win, tantalisingly one short of Mike the Bike's total. And I was feeling good and confident about the remaining tussles with the TT's top dogs, mega-winner John McGuinness, Michael Dunlop and Bruce Anstey.

It was odd, because I had been expecting a few other people to be doing the same – but they didn't and that was strange. But I also reckoned that racing the TT had gone to the next level. You ride the bike short-circuit style a lot of the time nowadays. We use a good deal of wheel spin and slide around, things that you never used to do around the island's circuit, a big change in riding style.

After that win in the Superstock race Philip Neill was as chuffed as can be, rejoicing: 'Obviously it was not for the want of trying with our big efforts over the last few years – and this is probably the most satisfying victory as we are in a new relationship with BMW – and it is our first win for Tyco as a sponsor.

'It is really, really important for us Neills and I have to confess it is not just for me and it is not for my father... it is for the boys throughout the entire team. Every one of them is so important because they get us to the start line by doing a great job. And we have just seen a superb display from Hutchy.'

And it did not end there. I was not content to be stuck on thirteen wins, I really wanted to hit the fourteen mark to earn equal status with Hailwood, who had set the target with his 1979 victory on his last amazing TT appearance at the age of forty.

It happened in the second Supersport TT on the Team Traction Control Yamaha R6. Ever since I started to ride for them they have been behind me all the way, and having them on my side has been of great benefit to me. At the North West 200, before the TT, we had a few setbacks – but then in the first practice session on the island, when I managed six laps on the YZFR6 Yamaha, I loved it. There were some hitches, with sessions red-flagged, so I didn't really get a chance for a real go on the bike in preparation for the Supersport race. To say I was a wee bit nervous on the morning of the first race is an understatement. But I need not have fretted. The Yamaha performed perfectly and answered all my demands on it without missing a beat. It was beautiful and memorable racing around in that great weather on that little bike, which was so responsive and easy to ride. Just terrific. Another win. And now only Joey Dunlop, John McGuinness and Dave Molyneux have won more TTs than I have, leaving me joint fourth (with Hailwood) on the all-time winners' list. I can hardly believe it, considering that, crucially, I had four of my best years off.

But what an honour. To be ranked alongside illustrious names like those is a feeling that I can hardly explain. For me, winning for a third time that week was a never-to-be-forgotten achievement: I had drawn level with Hailwood's record. It is, even now, astonishing, and such a momentous privilege, to be mentioned in the same breath as him, and I definitely did not want to hang around on the thirteen-wins figure. I was having so much fun again – just like 2010 – and I couldn't wait to get back into the fray. That's how upbeat and raring to go I was.

My win on the Wednesday was my fourth in a row on a 600cc and my eighth in total, which made me the most successful Supersport competitor at the mid-summer event. As well as that, it finished off a very satisfying run of Supersport and Superstock results with a treble for the second year running.

But it didn't all get off to the required start, which was delayed due to mist and overnight downpours that messed up circuit conditions enough for us to have to hang around until they improved. And even then it was dodgy; there was most certainly less grip and I could feel it on the front end. It had rained so hard that all the rubber had washed away, making it impossible to run quite as quick all around the track. I thought at first I had a puncture, but it was just a trick of the conditions – and, really, the bike was in faultless nick and giving me a perfect ride.

The specialist bike-racing critics wrote that the 2016 TT series would always be remembered for the confrontations between me and Michael Dunlop. We arrived on the island with eleven wins each and were each well aware of the other's dedication to adding to the number, to the cost of either one of us. I said then that I thought only Michael and I, both multiple winners, were trying seriously to win five races. I'd notched my treble in 2015, my first real go at the TT since my five wins in 2010 on the Padgett Honda. Michael had won four races in 2013 and did it all again the following year. The rivalry between us must have been a treat for the fans, even if it was tough going for the two of us. I did make the point, which didn't go down too well, that Michael had done all his winning while I was out of action because of my injuries.

After my win on Wednesday, when we had renewed our tussle in the second Supersport race, the first three bikes home were stripped down, with a focus on my machine. But the organisers blew away any suspicions by issuing a release which emphasised: 'No discrepancies were identified in any one of the motorcycles checked.' A question had been raised – by whom? – regarding the pistons on my R6, although they were found to comply with the regulations. It was later explained that a TT official – unnamed – had uttered 'an inappropriate comment' and that had activated the process of investigation. No official protest was made – but for some reason best known to himself Michael Dunlop referred to the issue after he had clinched the Senior TT later in the week. He was quoted as saying: 'I got a bit peeved by something that happened on Wednesday and I came out today to make amends.' I responded that I had done nothing but compliment Michael all week.

As we built up to the race week we had a real neck-and-neck battle on our S1000RRs. In practice I was first to clock a plus-130mph lap on my Superbike at 131.574. Then, the following evening, Michael topped the 132 mph mark. We were all set for a ding-dong. And that's the way it turned out, another thriller of a week for spectators and riders alike.

Friday afternoon's Senior went all Dunlop's way with me second and McGuinness third. Michael and I were both on equally matched and superb BMWs. I cracked the 133 mph lap bracket – but then Michael, pulling out all the stops, topped that with another outright lap record of 133.962 mph to help him hold on to his lead for his second six-lap race win of the week.

So you can tell that we were at it hammer and tongs. I can reveal that I had opted to run my Superstock-spec S1000RR engine instead of the more powerful Superbike unit for the Senior showdown because of the way the Superbike engine delivered its power. And, sure, it had a faultless run in the race, but to be honest that was a mistake, the wrong decision in terms of winning the race. But these mistaken judgements do happen. And when you find the odds are against you, you just have to give it your best shot. Which I did. In the end, however, the bike wasn't quite up to my aims for it. I knew we'd be lacking in speed with the Superstock engine, but I felt I could ride the bike just how I wanted. I did the best I could for every yard of the six laps – but we were beaten.

McGuinness, third on the Honda, said: 'Hutchy came past me into Parliament Square and I got a tow. It taught me a few things about how to ride even faster at the TT. Hutchy was leaning over further, braking later and getting on the gas earlier. I dropped in behind him and he dragged me on a bit. But, wow, was he pushing hard! It just goes to show, I am forty-four and fat but with a great record around here – but you are never too old to learn.'

He also said, cheeky bugger that he is: 'The easiest thing Hutchy could have done at the time of his injury was to have his leg whipped off and fit a prosthetic, and knowing him he would still have gone on to be an Olympic gold medallist. He is a winner. Not the most gifted – but very driven.'

The uniqueness of the TT is a magnet for all of who revel in a challenge right on and, sometimes, over the edge. I respect the event. It would be foolish not to – idiotic in fact – and there have been those who have fallen into the trap of taking one risk too many and suffering the resultant consequences, fatally in some instances, permanently damaging physically or mentally in others. That is why it is crucial to remind yourself that not only triumph, but survival, are dependent on the alliance of skill, awareness and down-to-earth common sense. There is both a magic and a mystery cloaking what is the ultimate and supreme test of man, machine and back-up team. The sheer aura of the festival, an annual date with daring with its erratic moods of, say, sudden and blinding sunshine around a bend in the road that is awash from a downpour, or finding the Mountain shrouded in a curtain of mist, can very easily trick you into doing something not akin to good judgement. That is why it is vital to look clear-eyed at its challenge, to avoid landing yourself in a lethal predicament, and with the constantly threatening chance of taking a rival down to disaster along with yourself.

Mike Hailwood, who won GPs all over the place and world titles with them, always insisted to Ted Macauley, his good friend and manager and organiser of Mike's sensational return to the TT in 1978, that there was no feeling of utter and complete satisfaction to equal that of winning around the island's famous, and infamous, circuit against a hundred or so guys in the same race with the same towering intent. Across the decades, he said he had seen too many families and friends who had been left to mourn the loss of a loved one, a fully committed TT racer, so often trapped into taking one chance too many, stretching his ability beyond its limits in a reflex action rather than coolly weighing up the odds. But, Mike added, 'I don't suppose you can really help yourself if you are a real competitor driven by the urge to win.'

From my own point of view, even throughout my long and painful recovery from injury, I do not believe that my keenness to get back on a bike in the island faltered for one fraction of a second. I was more anxious to make up for lost time than worried or fearful about not making it back to race at the TT, or anywhere else for that matter.

I am often asked if there was ever a turning point after my injuries, a time when I realised I was once more fit enough to race? The answer is no. It was just a progression. I simply tried to ride as often as I could, whether helping with instruction on track days or taking off to Spain to put in some track time. As long as I was on a bike I was happy. And it went a long way to rebuilding my confidence, as well as, in a practical sense, to my getting used to the right-hand-side gear shift because my left leg was such a wreck.

After I won those five TT races in 2010 I was constantly

asked if I was going to be dissatisfied by achieving anything less. Again, the answer is no. I would be disappointed at not winning again in a week's racing there – but as long as I satisfy myself that I have put in all the effort I can, even without a win, and am prepared to work on why I failed in order to ensure that I do better next time, then I am content.

It is, I know, difficult for people to understand, but winning my comeback in the opening Supersport race in 2015 after all the doubt and pain my injuries had provoked meant more to me than winning all five of those races in 2010. It was that special. Proof to myself that I had got back to where I wanted to be: fully fit for the job.

What I did find, however, and as I mentioned earlier, was that in taking on the TT nowadays the style of riding has changed, and increasingly you ride it in short-circuit fashion. There's loads of wheelspin and slides all over the place, things that never used to happen in days gone by. It used to be that the bike was always in line – but these days you are almost floating into the corners, going much quicker and really attacking them, rather than aiming for the perfect line, and that has all developed from short-circuit racing. Still, that's okay with me, and I guess with most of the other guys, too.

I'd like to come back to a mention of the Tyco BMW team. Racing with them in the 2016 TT, my first on the Tyco BMW after a year on the Paul Bird Motorsport Kawasaki ZX-10R, was truly great. They did a fantastic job and the bike was faultless, suffering not a single breakdown. I just loved riding it, not least because it is such a superb ride that I never had to push out of my comfort zone. It would a real treat to stay on a BMW for next year because I've had three manufacturers in three years and getting back to racing for wins after my injury means that I need a level of consistency to ensure I have a good chance of climbing the top step of the podiums.

As ever, the 2016 TT had its dramas, including my falling-out with Michael Dunlop, but that rather messy interlude can take nothing away from my overall delight at my results and my speeds, with a restored confidence that will only get even stronger and stronger in my pursuit of more success.

Really, it was thanks to the absolute expertise of the surgeons that what could have been a disastrous end to my career was raised from the depths, and not only am I still around today but I have been lucky enough to continue winning races. It took a long time and thirty operations and tested my resolve to its limits. But my well-placed trust in their ability in the end overcame fear and desperation and boosted me to a high level of confidence. That carried me through to not just my physical recovery but to the recovery of my motorcycle-racing abilities.

CHAPTER 11

THE ULSTER GP 2016

To discover in yourself a soaring level of achievement that you can barely believe you are blessed with has to be a benefit of rare reward.

And when, through your own efforts and ability, you are hailed as a history-maker and record-breaker, and seemingly endless adulation and accolades are heaped upon you, it is a humbling experience that it is almost impossible to imagine could be happening to you. Yet all of this happened to me after I followed up my extremely satisfying 2016 TT week with a mind-blowing streak at the Ulster Grand Prix, one of my favourite road-race circuits.

I won four races in a day, set a new lap record and was hailed as the quickest road racer on the planet. It was all headline stuff. The *Belfast Telegraph* duly blazed my name across its pages: 'Ian Hutchinson has been referred to as the Bionic Man and the Renaissance Kid – and now The World's Fastest Road Racer has been added to his CV after setting the Ulster Grand Prix alight with a new outright lap record of 134.089 mph.'

The day after my thirty-seventh birthday I set about celebrating in my own special way. The 7.4 mile (11.9 kilometre) Dundrod circuit on closed-off public roads around County Antrim is my kind of race. It used to be the stage for the RAC Tourist Trophy for sports cars between 1950 and 1955, and for the motorcycle grand prix from 1953 onwards. Famed car racer Mike Hawthorn, who liked to compete wearing a bow tie, set the lap record with a speed of 4 minutes 42 seconds, an average of 94.67 mph, in his D-type Jaguar in 1955. I went round the world's fastest race-track in 3 minutes 18.704 seconds. 'The Bingley Bullet stole the show,' the *Belfast Telegraph* added, very flatteringly.

Motor Cycle News joined in the back-patting with their own headline: 'Hutchy Batters Road Rivals as Records Tumble'.

In the event, what I did was save my best to last. I topped Bruce Anstey's 133.977-mph lap record, set by the New Zealander in 2010, with a final flying lap of the second Superbike race on my way to the last of four wins in the week. And, to be honest, I don't believe I have ever ridden as well around Dundrod. I have to say that I found it really hard to take it all in. When I was so badly injured and recovering the Ulster GP was the race I was away from most of all. But it was always a place where I gave a good showing. It had been tough to get back to the top, and to finish the season with a Superbike win on the open roads for Tyco BMW was the best thing ever for me. Their bikes, their backing and expertise and enthusiasm have been phenomenal.

MCN reported that after two difficult days of wet and foggy practice Saturday's race day lived up to all the hype, and the Irish fans were treated to one of the finest high-speed road-race shows ever seen at the Ulster GP. In the Superbike races Anstey on the Padgett's Honda RC213V-S got really stuck in with Conor Cummins, Peter Hickman and Dean Harrison poised to cash in on any errors by us up front. I scraped home, winning both races by 1 second ahead of Anstey, with Dunlop third. It was all phew-action! And in the Superstock battle I beat Michael Dunlop, the leader for most of the race, to the line by the merest margin of 0.2 seconds.

It was equally as tense in the second Supersport race, in which I had one hell of a tussle with William Dunlop, Michael's elder brother. He led for most of the race and I guess he looked like the winner, to the partisan Irish crowd's delight. But I opted to chance it and give it a go, and at Quarry Bends on the final lap I made my move and passed him, giving him no time to hit back. What a day!

When you are racing so fast in such a bloody tight, shoulder-to-shoulder melee you can get blinded a bit through the corners, particularly when you are following somebody. But as long as you are confident about your ability you just have to believe that what you are doing is right to get you ahead, and if successful, then defend as hard as you can to prevent anybody getting by you.

Any reader might reasonably ask: 'So what was it like riding flat-out, bike-to-bike at such blistering speeds over a track as threateningly dangerous as Dundrod?' The honest answer is that I have no concerns about competing barely inches apart from the likes of Bruce Anstey and the Dunlops at 190 mph in the Ulster's mass-start races. I would be happy to ride against guys like that all day long. I like all the action, close fought as it is and as it was at the Ulster in 2016. It is furious and frantic – but clean. We are all well aware of the risks and what the outcome of a crash at those speeds might be, but all the passing is clean and nobody... well, hardly anybody... will chance a desperate and dangerous move. You know that generally the guys you are up against and those closest to you in full-blooded commitment are not going to do anything unusual or stupid.

In my record-busting Ulster Grand Prix I gave it my all. So did everybody else. The result was incredibly fast, close racing, a fitting finale to my memorable 2016 road-race season. All I have to do now is do it all over again. And I will most certainly be giving it my all until the day I finally hang up my leathers. It's the only way I know . . . and I just hope I can add to the record books a few more times before I have to become an envious trackside spectator.

PENPIX

The unique quality of the TT and the distinct challenge it poses has triggered the fascinating development of road-race specialists, including me, whose varying ages defy the generally argued logic that motorbike racing, particularly on open-road tracks like the Isle of Man and the North West 200, should be the preserve of competitors at the younger end of the scale.

The separation between the eternally memorable and the instantly forgettable is the briefest reflex action in the madcap melee of a charge of hell-bent racers, some riding at close to 200 mph, approaching an unwary bunch of 50 mph slower guys. In that blink of an eye races are won or lost, or painful disaster ensues.

We, me included, have all taken ourselves close, very

close, to the edge of survival in committed effort to emerge victorious in the toughest of all races. So here I have listed a line-up of men who have stirred themselves to those towering levels in the past and show few signs of failing to climb the heights in the near future. In other words, as long as I am giving it my all over the Mountain these riders will be ambitious to make my life at speed a total misery, and all of them have the ability to do just that . . . as I have found often enough to my cost, despite whatever full-out determination I may have put in to leave them in my wake and become the TT's all-time record winner.

Top of the list is Morecambe's John McGuinness, nicknamed 'King of the Mountain', now aged forty-four but with no signs of slowing down and by 2016 on twenty-three victories and forty-five podiums from eighteen TT festivals. He made his island debut in 1996, and his first win was the 1999 Lightweight 250 race. Last year, 2015, after his stunning Senior victory and new outright lap record, the former bricklayer turned pro racer joined Hailwood as an RAC Segrave medallist for his TT exploits. His ambition is to top legend Joey Dunlop's twenty-six-win record before he quits.

Next comes Bruce Anstey, the quiet man from New Zealand, now forty-seven, a winner in the island eleven times with thirty-six podiums. His IOM debut was in 1996 aboard a Yamaha when he finished twenty-ninth but retired in the Senior. His opening TT triumph was in 2002 in the

250cc race and he became a lap-record holder at 132.298 mph in the 2014 Superbike event. He says he was inspired to become a TT racer after watching Hailwood's winning comeback in 1978.

Ryan Farquhar, aged forty, is another gifted Northern Irish motorbike racer with three wins around the famous 37¾ mile course. Twelve podiums, too, from eleven TT festivals. The Dungannon veteran's opening victory was in the 2004 Production 600cc race. That cancelled out his reputation as one of the best riders *never* to have won a TT, despite breaking the lap record in the 600cc class in 2003. He did decide to quit in 2012 but returned to the fray in 2014, although only to compete in the Lightweight event. However, in 2016, he was again on a full factory Superbike with my team, Tyco BMW.

Another in his forties is Michael Rutter, the West Midlander nicknamed 'The Blade'. On top of his tremendous eight wins at the Macau Grand Prix, a total not matched by any other rider, he has run up four victories and fourteen podiums at the TT, and in 2015, hit a lap of 131.09 mph, his fastest time around the Mountain course. In 2012 he missed out on a £10,000 prize to be awarded to the first rider to lap at 100-plus mph on an electric bike because his 102.50 mph was achieved in practice and not during a race. He is a cool-headed, deep-thinking rider, not the most spectacular, but never panicked into rash moves. Racing is in his blood; his father, Tony, won seven TTs and was four times world champion in the TT F2 series in the 1970s.

Gary Johnson, thirty-five, who made his TT debut in 2007, stamped his authority and established himself as a looming threat by beating superstar John McGuinness and Guy Martin for his opening win on the island in 2011. He was a winner again in the Supersport class in 2014. His lap of 130-plus mph, on what he stresses is his favourite circuit, confirmed him as a deserving member of the TT elite.

A fast-rising talent at the younger end of my list of riders to look out for is lanky Manxman Conor Cummins, thirty, who was born in TT week 1986. He turned pro in 2006 and ran in his first TT that year. He has competed in nine events in the island without a win – but with a very promising four podiums. And he underpinned his precocious talent by lapping at 131.76 mph in 2015.

I have written elsewhere of Michael Dunlop, and the Dunlop family dynasty of road racers, with TT glory always in the offing, is doubled with Michael's thirty-year-old brother William, son of the late Robert, an accomplished racer, and nephew of Joey, who needs no introduction. He started racing at just seventeen on a 125cc. The Ballymoney Boy has raced in nine TTs, the first one in 2006, so far without a top finish. But his promise is underpinned with five podiums, one of them a third place.

At just twenty-five, James Hillier is another fast mover with the potential to be a regular winner. The Hampshire flyer had his first taste of the TT in 2008 and he was an impressive ninth in the Senior to win the Newcomer's Trophy. He has had one win since, the Lightweight in 2013, with six podiums – and has now switched to bigger Kawasakis. He has finished all five of his TTs inside the top twenty.

Mark my words, every one of these guys is equipped with the all-round ability to take the TT by storm, making the experience difficult for each other and, at the same time, thrilling spectators to the utmost in the long-standing tradition of the showcase TT.

POSTSCRIPT: WHAT NEXT?

My appreciation of and esteem for hard racers – guys like me, basically – fills me with a seemingly never-ending resolve to win at all costs. It is a feeling that never goes away, that's why I have not put a time limit on when I might pack up. I don't see any point in doing that – I'll do what's necessary when I sense the situation is ripe. You never know what is going to come along, do you? I've just gone from doom and gloom to now looking forward to the best years of racing I have ever had. I don't think you can see what's coming in the future; you might have one year where you are riding for a team and you are forty years old and fed up and it's not going right, and then something comes along and you can't wait to go again. I think it's just one of those sports where you have to take each year as it comes, and I believe you will know instinctively when the time is right to hang up your helmet and leathers.

As for, say, getting married, I have to admit that I am terrible in relationships. I get so deeply absorbed in my racing, and my life is so purely about my job, that I struggle to find breakaway time. Obviously, at the right time I hope I can do the right thing and look after a partner and take holidays and stuff, like all good husbands. But pretty much every single day of my life I am going round the Isle of Man TT in my head and it's hard to break away from it. And then, as I have found in past relationships, when I start to think that something is getting in the way of my work, that tends to be the end of it.

So overall the absolute absorbing factor is racing. To the dismissal of most other things . . . well, of everything else, really. So how do I relax?

It's an effort. l can remember going testing for four days in Marbella, Spain. A lovely place to sit back, sunbathe and relax. Most guys' dream trip. Work and play. Not me. Work! I went up to the track, and it started raining and I was unloading my own bike as soon as I could. I revelled in the first session and couldn't wait to have another three days on my bike. It wasn't so much being in Spain that was the problem, it was being away from riding.

There is, however, one idea that I struggle with: I don't want to drag racing on for years and become an old man competing and losing, because that would be an embarrassment.

If I can't be a winner, that will definitely stop me. But then, also, I am going to have to find something else to do because staying with my parents, and yes, living out in Spain like they do, I couldn't cope with getting out of bed and then doing nothing every day. I would have to have a job in Spain of some description. That's what scares me a little bit. What on earth am I going to do after I quit? I will only, hopefully, be halfway through my life when I finish racing. What can I do for the rest of it? You get used to the good life and all that goes with it. I am sure that having to give up a luxury lifestyle that you have grown familiar with can be a major problem. You get used to having a lot of things that would be much harder to acquire if you are not earning the right money. Leisure time counts, and you want to fill your spare time with what you enjoy, maybe buying seven- or eight-thousand-pound road bikes and expensive mountain bikes to help fill in all those gaps in your life, continuing to do what you enjoy most as relaxation.

And that's one thing I will want to go on doing. If all my mates are going out biking, I will meet younger riders and hang around with them, as I do with ex-racers, James Whitham and other former pros whose company and friendship I have come to enjoy over the years. Of course, I would want the most modern and pricey motocross and trials bikes and that takes some doing too, when you are no longer getting them for free or loaned to you, unless you are lucky enough to be able to afford to buy them.

But for now and the foreseeable future I shall go on doing what I love best: racing motorcycles on circuits like the Isle of Man's Mountain course – and winning.